# GEORGE OPPEN

New Collected Poems

George Oppen, Deer Isle, Maine, 1970

# GEORGE OPPEN

## New Collected Poems

Edited with an introduction and notes by

MICHAEL DAVIDSON

Preface by Eliot Weinberger

A NEW DIRECTIONS BOOK

The holograph manuscript materials on p. li and p. 351 are reproduced courtesy of the George Oppen Papers,
Mandeville Special Collections Library, University of California, San Diego, and are located respectively in
UCSD 16, 23, 11 and UCSD 16, 23, 15. The photographs on p. ii and pp. 287–88 are reproduced courtesy of
the Mary Oppen Papers, Mandeville Special Collections Library, University of California, San Diego; the first
is located in UCSD 16, 19, FB-108, the others in UCSD 16, 9, FB-094.

Manufactured in the United States of America
Book design by Sylvia Frezzolini Severance
New Directions Books are printed on acid-free paper
First published clothbound by New Directions in 2002
and as New Directions Paperbook (NDP1121) in 2008
Published simultaneously in Canada by Penguin Books Canada Limited

Library of Congress Cataloging-in-Publication Data

Oppen, George. 1908-1984
    New collected poems / George Oppen ; edited with an introduction and notes
by Michael Davidson ; preface by Eliot Weinberger.
    p. cm.
    Includes bibliographical references and index.
    cloth: ISBN 0-8112-1488-5 (alk. paper)
    paper: ISBN 0-8112-1805-4 (alk. paper)
    I. Davidson, Michael, 1944-  II. Title

PS3529.P54 A17 2002
811'.52—dc21                                    2001044048

New Directions Books are published for James Laughlin
by New Directions Publishing Corporation,
80 Eighth Avenue, New York, NY 10011

# CONTENTS

## THE MATERIALS (1962)

## THIS IN WHICH (1965)

## MYTH OF THE BLAZE (1972-1975)

## PRIMITIVE (1978)

## UNCOLLECTED PUBLISHED POEMS

## LIST OF ILLUSTRATIONS

# Preface:

# OPPEN THEN

Neither pedagogical nor oracular, more preoccupied with questions than answers, George Oppen was nonetheless surrounded by young writers in the 1960s and 1970s as a model—an impossibly inimitable model—of how to be a poet in shifting, disastrous, and what seemed to be apocalyptic times. He had an aura about him, that of the honorable man trying to speak in the roar of history, much like the aura that has now gathered posthumously around Paul Celan.

There were, first of all, the facts of his life, which had particular resonance in the era of the Vietnam War and of hectically mutating events and values. A product of the 1930s, Oppen had spent the first years of that decade attempting to rally a second generation of American modernism, relocated from Europe to the American city, that would continue and modify the poetic principles of its immediate predecessors while rejecting their political principles: a poetry that might not be for the masses, but one that did not loathe them. He had published a tiny book of enigmatic poems in 1934, then had joined the Communist Party and stopped writing. He was perhaps the only Party writer, anywhere, who had never written stirring doggerel or prose propaganda; who both had doubted the efficacy of poetry in hungry times and had resisted the Party's manipulation of the arts; who had believed that the proper role of a Party member was no different for a writer or a factory worker, that the work to be done was agitation and organization, in which poetry could have no place without compromising itself. Oppen's silence was political and not personal, ideological and not "writer's block," and not, as Hugh Kenner famously suggested, a mere glitch in time until the next poem. It had lasted twenty-five years, and it hung over us—young writers adrift in trying to respond, wondering if it was possible to respond adequately and usefully to the present in which we found ourselves—like the extreme act of a saint. We too had the faith, but would we be willing to stand silently for twenty-five years to prove it?

Moreover, in a time of war, and our pragmatic attempts to avoid it individually and utopian attempts to end it collectively, there was George Oppen, who had fought and had been seriously wounded as an infantryman in World War II, perhaps the only enduring American poet to participate in ground combat since the Civil War, the only one who knew firsthand: "Wars that are just? A simpler question: In the event, will you or will you not want to kill a German." (A question, it should be noted, without a question mark.) Then, in the 1950s, in the loathsome Cold War that warped our childhoods, he had been the only hero, of sorts, among American poets: Forced out of the country by McCarthyism and the House Un-American Activities Committee, he was in exile for seven years, avoiding the inevitable summons to "name names." Oppen's martyrdom, though less severe, was the left-wing counterpart to Ezra Pound's simultaneous, more disputable right-wing martyrdom in St. Elizabeths. Both, strangely, were allowed to return home in the same summer of 1958.

Added to this political romance was a personal one that seemed equally radical and unattainable as we ourselves fell in and out of love: his apparently blissful relationship with Mary, from whom he had been inseparable since age eighteen, fighting the good fight for art and justice. They always spoke in the first-person plural. They were their own little collective: "old" people who lived as we did, with random and shabby furniture, and moreover believed, as we did, that youth was on the verge of saving the world. They had even attended the notorious Altamont rock festival, when hippie love & peace turned into Hell's Angels violence—an event that seemed emblematic at the time—and shared the general disillusionment: Oppen's poem about it (in "Some San Francisco Poems") ends with the word "mourning."

Oppen's return to writing and publishing in the 1960s coincided with the miraculous emergence of an entire lost generation—Charles Reznikoff, Lorine Niedecker, Louis Zukofsky, Carl Rakosi and, in England, Basil Bunting—who for varying reasons had been invisible since the 1930s, and who suddenly appeared among us, now transformed into Venerable Sages. [George always seemed ancient, and I am shocked as I now calculate that he was only in his late fifties when I met him. That this was not merely an adolescent perspective is confirmed by photographs: in them, his gaunt and geological face makes him look twenty years older than his contemporaries.] All of these elders enlarged the possibilities of poetry—in a moment when there was an exhilarating racket of new ideas—but only Oppen, among them, spoke directly to the political consciousness and the political crisis of the time. In 1968, amidst the powerful (and still powerful) overtly political poems being written by Robert Duncan, Denise Levertov, Amiri Baraka, Allen Ginsberg, and so many others, it was Oppen's *Of Being Numerous* that, from its opening words, struck me, still a teenager, as the poetry that had captured the interior essence of where we are, who we are, right now:

> There are things
> We live among 'and to see them
> Is to know ourselves'.

These lines are now philosophical, but they were once political, for then the things we lived among included the first televised scenes of war and the photographs of napalmed children: Was seeing them seeing ourselves? Over and over Oppen emphasized that the function of poetry was a test of truth; he may have been the last writer in the West to use the word "truth" without irony. For him, "So much depends upon a red wheelbarrow" was a moral statement, with "wheelbarrow" both a thing and a word. The poet's task was to restore meaning to words—particularly in a time of official lies—and this was only possible through direct experience of the words themselves. Speaking of H.D., he once asked, in amazement, "How can you write a word like 'angel'?" Words, he said, had to be "earned"; words were "frightening."

Oppen's standard, his obsession, was "honesty" in the poem, Pound's ideogram of a man standing by his word. He insisted on writing only about what he himself had seen, and the act of seeing them: The angels he had mentioned in a poem were the ones in the windows of Chartres. [This insistence also created an obstinate blindness to all forms of surrealism, which he saw as an escape from, and not a way into, current realities.] Uniquely among American poets, there are almost no mythological references and no myth-making, no exotica, no personae, only one or two passing historical references, and almost no similes in his work: in Oppen's world, things are not "like," they are there, right in front of you, and there with an exclamation point. His metaphor for "seeing" in a poem is apocalyptic: the man in the ditch, staring at the spinning wheels of his overturned car—as he himself, in his youth, had been the driver in a fatal crash. Until very late, and unusually for an avant-gardist, he capitalized the first letter of every line: poetry was too powerful to trivialize with lower case.

Curiously, Oppen's struggle for "clarity"—another favorite word—did not result in the kind of small perfection of unadorned speech achieved by Reznikoff and Niedecker, poems that reached what Zukofsky called "total rest." Oppen's poems represent the struggle itself, and he continually rewrote them, cutting out and pasting words on top of other words, as though he were a mason building a brick wall. But they are not brick walls. They are often abstract, as mysterious as koans, a sea-surge of contradictory forces: assertions and their negations, declarations couched in double negatives, questions without answers, straightforward observations placed next to gnomic statements whose beauty lingers forever because they are never fully understood. It takes work—especially with the later poems—to read them aloud, for their arrangement on the page seems to function at cross-purposes to their sound: pauses in the middle of lines, syntactical endings and beginnings in the same line, enjambments across stanza breaks, inexplicable starts and stops, multiple possibilities of emphasis, phrases hanging. A late Oppen is like one of those Taoist rocks, full of holes, through which the breath, the force of the poem, circulates.

He wrote short poems and series of short poems, and what is

remarkable is that nearly any of the short poems could have been placed in one of the series, any of the series poems could have been a separate short poem, and almost none of them can stand alone as self-contained "anthology pieces." Much like Celan, all of Oppen's work—though this was not his intention, though he was not writing a long and life-long poem like Pound or Olson—seems to belong to a single continuing poem, a poem that now includes those, collected here for the first time, that were in magazines but omitted from his books, or not published at all. It is a poem that returns again and again to the same things: the Middle English western wind, Blake's Tyger, the boats of Maine, people in cars, his foxhole in the war, Mary's beauty, Robinson Crusoe, city walls, city streets, crowds, the young, tools, ditches, glass, and the words "little" and "small." His universe was an "immense heap of little things" (Coleridge) and in his quest for truth, he believed that the little things and the little words—pronouns, articles, prepositions, short declarative sentences—were the truest, yet even they had to be taken apart and sometimes left unreassembled.

He may never be the subject of a biography, for his life beyond its outline remains a mystery, and for decades left no paper trail. George and Mary had carefully edited the story, and always told the same anecdotes, all of which are in Mary's autobiography, *Meaning a Life*, the only sustained work of Objectivist prose, and all of which had a quality of wonder like the children's books they loved: the young couple in 1928, sailing in a small boat across the Great Lakes, down the Erie Canal and into the Hudson River to New York City (a dreamlike voyage that always reminded me of the trolley ride into the city in Murnau's exactly contemporary film, *Sunrise*); their anachronistic travels by horse and buggy through France; the rent strike in Queens where they flushed plaster of Paris down the toilets and turned the plumbing into a tree of stone. . . But among the untold stories is the enigma that hangs over Oppen, more impenetrable than his long silence: his relation, in mind perhaps more than deed, to Communism as it evolved. Unlike Neruda or Hikmet or MacDiarmid, it is impossible to imagine George—this man of questions, unsentimentally devoted to honesty, truth, and honor—as a Stalinist. He was always evasive on this subject; no one even knows when he left the Party.

He had lived as a boy next door to D.W. Griffith. He spoke softly and had a certain accent, most notable in its r's, common to cultivated New York Jews of his generation, that has now almost completely vanished. Though his poems rarely have any humor, he himself was very funny, and he would punctuate his wisecracks with a bobbing of his prominent eyebrows that was identical to Groucho Marx. He and Mary were nomadic for most of their lives, living on boats or in hotels or trailers or cheap apartments communally with other couples and families; his whole life was in resolute flight from a wealthy childhood. He tried, and it is not easy, to live "honorably"—his word—as an American poet: he never taught writing or served on any literary panels or juries or committees; he wrote only one book review; and he largely refused to give readings after he won, to everyone's surprise, a Pulitzer. In his last years, there was a piece of paper pinned over his desk that read "Only one mistake, Ezra! You should have talked to women." The last public line he wrote was: "My happiness is the knowledge of all we do not know."

A life-long sailor, builder of his own small boats, when he appeared among us in the 1960s he seemed a shipwreck survivor, a returned Crusoe, who had lived through disaster and now saw the world more intently, who no longer had any answers, and struggled with the precise articulation of his uncertainties. Once, at my parent's house, an ancient friend of theirs came to visit and noticed a copy of a little magazine I had once edited: "George Oppen—I haven't heard that name for years! I never knew he wrote poetry."

ELIOT WEINBERGER

# Introduction

## "A MAN OF THE THIRTIES"

When George Oppen published his *Collected Poems* with New Directions in 1975, he remarked in a note that the book was

> created by childhood, by my mother's death, by New Rochelle and sail-boats, by marriage to Mary, by hitch-hiking across the country with no money, by the depression, by the political movement demanding relief for the unemployed and the hungry, by the second world war, by the Fascist Threat, by the childhood of our daughter, by our life in France and in Mexico. If I live long enough, I will have more to tell of, and to understand.[1]

Then in double unclosed parentheses he added "(((*If* I should write another Collected poems, I would be rather startled." Oppen did not live long enough to publish "another Collected poems," but if he were to see this reedited version he might be "rather startled" to find many poems that he published in magazines and journals but never included in his 1975 edition. Moreover, he might have been dismayed to see the addition of poems taken from manuscripts and working papers that he never intended to print at all. Oppen was not someone who approved of casual miscellany. He whittled and refined his poems into tough, recalcitrant lyrics that would endure the test of time. Furthermore, he embedded his lyrics in long series or sequences that show the chisel marks of their construction.[2] His oft-quoted version of Charles Reznikoff's lyric applies for his own work as well; he sought "the girder / Still itself among the rubble."[3] This new edition of his

*Collected Poems* may include a bit more of the "rubble" than Oppen would have liked.

My justification for these inclusions derives from the peculiar quality of Oppen's compositional method, his tendency to embed poems in the midst of a kind of *textual* rubble. He wrote on every sort of paper, both in longhand and by typewriter, with scribbled corrections, notes, and emendations filling every corner of the page. Drafts of poems appear on the same page as laundry lists, newspaper quotations, observations on current events, and architectural doodles. It is often difficult to discern where the poem ends and the "rubble" begins. Prose quotation is often transformed into lined verse; new lines are pasted on top of earlier lines and stick off the page like a relief map; drafts of poems are enclosed in folders joined with paper clips and pipestem cleaners; one manuscript is held together with a nail driven through the pages into a piece of wood. When Oppen speaks of his poetry as "[piling] up pieces of paper to find the words," he is not being metaphoric.

In reediting George Oppen's *Collected Poems* I have tried to respect the integrity of the poet's rigorous compositional standards by drawing from his uncollected and unpublished poems those which he worked on over a period of time or which elucidate other published poems. But I have also been moved by the first part of his remark above—that for Oppen, poems are forged out of social and familial forces beyond the aesthetic. "I am a man of the Thirties // 'No other taste shall change this'", he says in one of those poems he never collected.[4] Oppen felt that poetry needed to be tested against experience—in his case, that of the Depression, the threat of Fascism, working as a carpenter and sailor, raising a family—and no other taste or aesthetic discrimination should supersede these facts.[5] The experience of the 1930s convinced him that the aesthetic strategies of his modernist predecessors were no longer adequate to deal with the social trauma of increasing modernization. Yes, poems had to strive for a level of clarity and objectivity, but not as a way of escaping history through mythic universals or distancing personae. Rather, history had to be recreated within the poem, subjected to a language free from instrumental uses—a language "Geared in the loose mechanics of the world . . ."[6]

# "NO NARRATIVE BUT OURSELVES"[7]

That world began for George Oppen on April 24, 1908, in New Rochelle, New York. He was born the son of a successful businessman, George August Oppenheimer (the family name was changed to Oppen in 1927) and Elsie Rothfeld. His early years were spent in relative luxury, a fact that haunted him later in life as someone who identified with the working classes. But this bourgeois life offered him and his older sister Elizabeth (Libby) good schools, travel, and material comforts. His mother suffered from various mental problems and finally, following a nervous breakdown, committed suicide when Oppen was four. When Oppen was seven, his father married Selville Shainwald, a woman of considerable wealth and ambition. The boy's relationship with his stepmother was traumatic, however, involving forms of psychological and physical abuse that were to haunt him later in life.[8]

In 1918 a daughter, June Frances, was born to the couple. She would become a close intellectual and personal confidante of her half brother, someone who stayed within the family but identified with Oppen's leftist ideals. That same year, the family moved from New York to San Francisco, where Oppen's father ran a succession of movie houses. The Oppenheimers lived on San Francisco's fashionable Nob Hill, where George attended private schools. In 1926 he entered what is now Oregon State University at Corvallis where, in a course in modern poetry, he met his future wife, Mary Colby. On their first date, the couple stayed out all night, causing Mary to be expelled and George to be suspended from the college when they returned to campus the next day. It was a fortuitous, if calamitous, event, launching a relationship that would last for over fifty years and whose sustaining effect can be felt in many of Oppen's poems.

The couple left Oregon, where Mary's family lived, and began a period of itinerant work while hitching rides across the country. "Hitchhiking became more than flight from [George's] powerful family," Mary Oppen writes; "our discoveries themselves became an esthetic and a disclosure."[9] During their first hitchhiking trip, fearing police scrutiny while on the road, they were married in Dallas, Texas, on October 7, 1927. Oppen registered his name as "David Verdi." This bit of deception is described by Rachel Blau DuPlessis as offering them the illusion that they were not really married, "which seemed to give them a sense of continual and renewed choice in their deep commitment."[10]

The couple maintained a vagabond life, working for brief periods, writing poetry, and even submitting poems to local magazines. They settled for a time in San Francisco, where George worked in one of his father's theaters. The luxurious life of Nob Hill and conflicts with his father over money drove George and Mary out, and they hitchhiked to Detroit in 1928. There, they purchased a small catboat that they sailed through the Great Lakes to the Erie Canal and then to New York. Settling in Brooklyn, they met two poets who would exert a profound and lasting impact on Oppen's poetry, Louis Zukofsky and Charles Reznikoff. It was in their company that the plot for a new publishing venture was hatched, with Zukofsky as editor and Mary and George as publisher/printers. The name of the press was To Publishers, an abbreviation of "The Objectivists," but also celebrating function words like "to" and "the," upon which Objectivist aesthetics would be based.

1929 was an *annus mirabilis* for Oppen—the year of the great financial crash that inaugurated the Depression but, not coincidentally, also the year that he began writing the poems for his first book, *Discrete Series*. Oppen had just turned twenty-one, and he came into a small inheritance that permitted the couple to live, if marginally, at least free from financial anxieties:

> We were not absolutely free from the necessity to work (it might be said, since I worked now and then at the times that we needed more money). But we were absolutely free from the necessity of success.[11]

It was also in 1929 that they moved back to the San Francisco Bay area, settling in a house by the water in Belvedere, where they could indulge their love of sailing without living under the watchful eye of

George's family. It was as "Mr. George A. Oppen of Belevedere Cal" that Oppen published some of his first poems in *Poetry*, poems that were later included in *Discrete Series*. Although we tend to think of this seminal volume in early Objectivism as being generated within a New York environment, it is worth remembering that many of its poems were written in the shadow of the Golden Gate Bridge.

After their sojourn in California, and impatient to indulge their wanderlust further, the Oppens moved to Europe in 1929, and after traveling slowly from Le Havre through Paris to Marseilles, settled in Le Beausset, in the Var region of southern France. While there, they renewed their intention to publish books through To Publishers. With Zukofsky as editor in New York, they brought out Ezra Pound's *How to Read*, William Carlos Williams's *A Novelette and Other Prose (1921-1931)*, and Zukofsky's *An "Objectivists" Anthology*.[12] At the same time, Oppen sent poems to *Poetry* that appeared in the February 1931 "Objectivist" issue, a venture suggested to the editor by Pound. Pound had earlier received a manuscript of Oppen's poems from Zukofsky, who excused its stylistic peculiarities by speaking of the poet's particular way of managing a certain type of "void."[13] Pound was impressed enough with the manuscript (an early draft of *Discrete Series*) to offer to write a preface for the book.

Late in their sojourn in Europe the Oppens visited Pound in Rapallo, where the older poet lived with his wife, Dorothy. Pound had exerted a powerful influence on Oppen and had been generous in his support of the Objectivist movement in general. But from the outset, there were tensions. Walking on the waterfront of Rapallo, Pound, with a flourish, gestured toward the sea: "From there came the Greek ships," but Mary Oppen, in her memoir, *Meaning a Life*, comments that Pound was gesturing in the wrong direction, an indication that Pound was "too far away from [his] own roots." Respect for the poet and the difference in their ages "forbade our telling him that we lacked respect for his politics and that he should go home."[14] Although Pound's influence on the shape of Oppen's poetry endured, the older poet's embrace of Social Credit economics and Fascism gradually drove the poets apart for many decades until an emotional reunion in 1969.

The Oppens returned to New York in 1933, where they began a new publishing collective, The Objectivist Press. Charles Reznikoff, who was a lawyer, provided the press's unadorned publishing statement, which appeared on dust jackets of the books it produced: "The Objectivist Press is an organization of poets who are printing their own work and that of others they think ought to be printed."[15] This rather functionalist definition marks a certain reluctance to identify as a group along the lines of other modernist movements. Zukofsky, Oppen, and Reznikoff knew each other at the time, and they shared backgrounds as Jews from working-class, immigrant families. Zukofsky provided the terms for a shared poetics as the editor of the "Objectivist" issue of *Poetry*, which included his essay "Program: 'Objectivists' 1931." But the three principal members did not rally around a coherent program or manifesto. Rather, they saw themselves as outsiders to official American literary and political life and unique within their own cohort. As Kenneth Rexroth remarked, "Almost all the people Zukofsky picked as Objectivists didn't agree with him, didn't write like him or like one another, and didn't want to be called Objectivists."[16]

Among the several books published by the Objectivist Press (including Williams's *Collected Poems, 1921–31* and three books by Reznikoff) was Oppen's *Discrete Series* in 1934. Early drafts of the book are labeled "The 1930s," which suggests that in its initial formulation, the book was seen as a commentary on the historical period in which it was written. Pound wrote the preface as promised, but Williams's review of the book provided much clearer terms for its salient features: "[Oppen's] poems seek an irreducible minimum in the means for the achievement of their objective, no loose bolts or beams sticking out unattached at one end or put there to hold up a rococo cupid or a concrete saint, nor either to be a frame for a portrait of mother or a deceased wife."[17]

The appearance of this rather modest book, one poem per page, coincided with Oppen's increased commitment to issues of politics and social welfare brought about by the global Depression. Feeling that he could neither write poems in service to social causes nor sequester those causes in hermetic formalism, he stopped writing altogether for a twenty-five-year period, lasting from 1934 to 1958. The formation of the Popular Front in 1935 inspired Mary and George to join the Communist Party as part of its united stand against Fascism. Along with radicals, trade unionists, artists, and immigrants, they participated actively in relief efforts to obtain rent and food for people who had fallen on hard times. Oppen became the Communist Party's election campaign manager for Brooklyn in 1936. In that same year George and Mary were arrested at a sit-in at a neighborhood relief bureau while working for the Workers Alliance. The trial on the charge of felonious assault on the police took two years, and it wasn't until 1938 that they were acquitted. In 1937 they helped organize the Farmers' Union milk strike near Utica, New York. All of these events reappear throughout Oppen's work as talismanic signs of a vital commitment shared by the couple: "So we lived / And chose to live // These were our times." [18]

In the midst of their political work, and after several miscarriages, Mary gave birth to a baby girl, Linda Jean, in May of 1940. At that time, Oppen was training in a government-run school for pattern-makers. In the early years of World War II he worked for Grumman Aircraft on Long Island, hoping to earn the classification of pattern-maker in the Union of Machinists for work after the hostilities began. The family then moved to Detroit in 1942, where George continued working in the defense industry, but by changing jobs, he lost his military exemption and was shortly thereafter drafted into the army. George relocated to Louisiana in 1943 to do his military training, and when he shipped out, Mary and four-year-old Linda returned to New York for the duration of the war.

Oppen landed in Marseilles where he served with the 103rd Infantry Division in the Anti-tank Company of the 411th Infantry Regiment and moved north to participate in the Battle of the Bulge and afterward saw action in the mountainous region near Alsace. Late in the war, while he was driving a truck in a convoy, he came under enemy fire and was forced to dive into a foxhole. Two other men also leapt in the foxhole, and both were killed, while Oppen was seriously wounded from exploding shrapnel. In a later poem he remembers lying in the foxhole, pinned down by enemy gunfire and surrounded by carnage, remembering "Wyatt's / lyric and Rezi's / running thru my mind / in the destroyed (and guilty) Theatre / of the War..."[19] But if his thoughts were sustained by poetry, he was cautious enough to bury his dogtags, which would identify him to the nearby enemy as Jewish.[20]

The war ended in May 1945, and although Oppen was awarded a Purple Heart, he was not released to come home until the end of November. Upon returning to New York, he built a camping trailer and moved his family to the West Coast, living in the camper in northern California and Oregon and then settling in a trailer park in Compton. A year later they relocated to Redondo Beach, where the Oppens built a house. George and a partner built houses as part of the huge boom in housing following the war, and when he tired of that, he began a small cabinetmaking business. Although by the 1950s he had ceased being active in the Communist Party, his and Mary's political past was becoming a liability in the anti-Communist period of the early 1950s. Almost certain to be called for questioning before Joseph McCarthy's Senate investigative subcommittee or the House Un-American Activities Committee for their political work and worried about the disruption that such governmental harassment would bring to the life of their young daughter, the Oppens moved to Mexico City.[21]

In Mexico, George opened a furniture-making business with a partner. He and Mary enrolled in an art school and became active in a large expatriate community of intellectuals and artists who, like themselves, had fled the United States. The Mexico period appears to have been relatively peaceful, a result perhaps of their feeling that as leftist expatriates with a small child, it was best not to be too visible. But despite their distance from the United States, the Oppens were followed by Mexican authorities holding dossiers on the couple supplied by the CIA and FBI. Given this tense situation, Mary said that they "weren't living within our personalities and that was difficult for us." [22]

With the exception of a trip to Guatemala in 1951, the Oppens stayed close to home throughout their Mexican years. In 1958, however, restrictions on obtaining passports were eased, and they began to contemplate returning to the United States. Anti-Communist hysteria was beginning to wane, and their daughter, Linda, had enrolled at Sarah Lawrence College in September, 1958. Oppen began writing again, spurred on by a vivid dream in which he finds himself looking into his father's files and discovers one labeled, "How to Prevent Rust in Copper." He awoke laughing, knowing full well that copper does not rust. Upon hearing this dream later, his therapist reportedly said, "You were dreaming that you're going to rust." And Oppen reflected, said "thanks" and "went home and bought a ream of paper, and started to write." [23]

The first poem to mark the end of his twenty-five-year silence, composed while still in Mexico, was "Blood from the Stone," which he misdated in an early draft as "1949," suggesting a certain impatience to return into the world of poetry and to the United States after seven years of exile. The poem is a retrospective look at the period that had created that silence:

> The Thirties.  And
> A spectre
>
> In every street,
> In all inexplicable crowds, what they did then
> Is still their lives.[24]

In an earlier draft, the poem was titled "To Date," marking the importance of the 1930s in "dating" his generation. The specter of Communism that haunted Marx's 19th-century Europe returned for men and women of the left during the Depression, but as Eric Homberger observes, the meaning of the period for the Objectivists was more complicated than the fact that they participated in the Communist Party, USA. Understanding that period must take account of their struggles within Stalinization to maintain aesthetic values interpreted by the Party as bourgeois and elitist.[25] And it must take account of their Jewishness at a moment of increasing Fascism abroad. The silence that preceded the writing of "Blood from the Stone" was shared by all of the Objectivists; they remained marginal writers until the 1960s. But from Oppen's vantage in Mexico, there was something more to do in the country of his birth. As he shouts in the opening lines of "Blood from the Stone": "O! / Everything I am is / Us. Come home."

The Oppens did "come home" temporarily in November 1958, when they visited their daughter at Sarah Lawrence. They returned to Mexico several times in the next few years (including one trip with Louis Zukofsky and his family), living in Mexico City and then moving to Acapulco in 1959. A number of the poems included in *The Materials* were drafted during this period, and the landscape of Mexico can be seen in poems like "Resort" and "Coastal Strip." But by 1961, the Oppens had made a firm move back to New York City, where a new stage of Oppen's literary career began.[26]

The early 1960s in Brooklyn brought them fully back into the literary and cultural life of New York. While they renewed friendships with Zukofsky and Reznikoff and others of the older generation, they also met and formed new and important contacts with a younger generation of writers—David Antin, Jerome Rothenberg, Rachel Blau DuPlessis, Diane Wakoski, Armand Schwerner, John Crawford—that provided much-needed conversation and community. It was this group of poets whose magazines and reading venues provided a vital forum for Oppen's new reception. With the efflorescence of new poetic movements, defined by Donald Allen in his 1960 anthology, *The New American Poetry*, Oppen became somewhat of an elder statesman (although he was still in his fifties) for the Black Mountain, Beat, and other movements of the 1960s. Perhaps more importantly, he was genuinely interested in new writing and provided a sympathetic—or occasionally curmudgeonly—ear for younger poets in New York.

George and Mary visited the city's museums and art galleries, went to poetry readings, and absorbed a world of culture and literary conversation from which they had been removed for almost two decades. On a boat Oppen had built in Mexico City, they sailed during the summers in New England, especially around Little Deer Isle in Maine. There were trips to Europe in 1961 and 1962. In 1964, Oppen and David Ignatow gave a poetry reading for the Academy of American Poets at the Guggenheim Museum, introduced by William Meredith. Oppen also wrote one of his rare prose pieces, a review of Michael McClure, Allen Ginsberg, and Charles Olson for *Poetry*.[27]

The Oppens lived at 364 Henry Street, not far from Zukofsky in Brooklyn Heights, and although the two old friends continued to see each other, there was a general cooling of their relationship. Although the differences may have been temperamental, the split was aesthetic as well. However oblique his poems, George always felt that clarity was his primary goal: "I have not and never did have any motive of poetry / But to achieve clarity."[28] Oppen felt that Zukofsky used obscurity and incomprehensibility as a tactic, leaving the reader behind. "It doesn't matter, [readers] don't care if they understand you or not," Mary reports Zukofsky as having said.[29] Despite these differences, Oppen's letters to Zukofsky during this period reveal a continuing respect for his work and express interest in seeing a Zukofsky "Collected Poems" in print.

In 1962, Oppen published *The Materials* with New Directions in collaboration with the *San Francisco Review*. His sister June, who was then publishing *SFR* as a literary journal, joined forces with James Laughlin at New Directions and brought out, in addition to *The Materials*, Charles Reznikoff's *By the Waters of Manhattan* and William Bronk's *The World, the Worldless*. *The Materials* represents a transition from the Mexico period (many poems feature settings in Mexico City and Acapulco) to the United States. The book's epigraph from Jacques Maritain's *Creative Intuition in Art and Poetry* suggests the mood of transformation that Oppen felt by returning to poetry: "We awake in the same moment to ourselves and to things." It is a quotation that reinforces Oppen's longstanding attempt to synthesize a social ethos with material reality, to negotiate between the self and a world of objects. The quotation parallels Oppen's interest in Heidegger, another philosopher for whom truth can only be encountered among the things of the world. At the same time, it was an epigraph that describes a new "awakening" to a United States changed by Cold War tensions. Oppen's Marxist critique of capitalism had not diminished—to this extent the book's title refers to social as well as empirical materialism—but it was rethought within a world in which state capitalism and Communism seemed to merge in the context of a race for world domination. Poems like "Time of the Missile" and "The Crowded Countries of the Bomb" show that Oppen was deeply concerned about the mood of paranoia that pervaded the United States when tensions with the Soviet Union were at their highest point.

These same concerns animate Oppen's next collection, *This in Which*, published in the San Francisco Review Series with New Directions in 1966. It is a book that emphasizes Oppen's perception of increasing class disparity in the United States at a moment of extraordinary material prosperity. In "A Language of New York," Oppen observes:

> A city of the corporations
>
> Glassed
> In dreams
>
> And images—[30]

The idea of a world inoculated from experience becomes a key issue as the poet looks back to his own upbringing in a bourgeois household. He remembers with unease "the noise of wealth" that drove him out of San Francisco and the "great house / With its servants, // The great utensiled / House."[31] At the same time, he remembers his meeting with Mary and their first night together:

> Parked in the fields
> All night
> So many years ago,
> We saw
> A lake beside us
> When the moon rose.[32]

In later 1964 through March of 1965, the Oppens visited the Bahamas with June Oppen Degnan and returned to drive their amphibious car (which could be converted into a boat) from Miami back to New York. The Oppens continued to vacation in Maine and in the early summer of 1966 traveled to France and Belgium. Upon returning from Europe, they left Brooklyn and moved to San Francisco, where they lived at 2811 Polk Street, within sight of the bay and in the midst of the city's lively literary scene. Returning to the city of his upbringing seems to have been made easier by his parents' absence from it, his father having died in 1954.[33] Oppen became close to other local poets—Robert Duncan, Mark Linenthal, Frances Jaffer, Kathleen Fraser, and Josephine Miles—and met for the first time, Carl Rakosi, whose work he had known for many years. Rakosi had become friends with Ricardo and Marcia Hofer while visiting Oaxaca, Mexico, and it was at dinner at the Hofers where Oppen and Rakosi met in the early 1970s.

In 1968, he published his best-known book, *Of Being Numerous*, the title poem of which expands an earlier sequence, "A Language of New York," from *This in Which* and reflects the poet's opposition to the Vietnam War. Perhaps the most significant change in this long series is its extensive quotation from correspondence, conversations, books, and news articles to give vivid form to the theme announced by the poem's title. How is it possible, the poem asks, to be both unique and yet live as a social being? "We are pressed, pressed on each other," Oppen says; yet at the same time "We have chosen the meaning / Of being numerous" and must reconcile ourselves to a social contract. Although these were issues facing many during the turbulent late 1960s, they carried special resonance for a poet who had relinquished the singular in favor of the social totality in his earlier career.

*Of Being Numerous* achieved a far wider circulation than Oppen's previous books. It won the Pulitzer Prize for Poetry in 1969, giving him his first real taste of national fame. The previous year he and other Objectivists—Louis Zukofsky, Charles Reznikoff, and Carl Rakosi—had been invited to the University of Wisconsin, Madison, where they were interviewed by L.S. Dembo, a professor of modern American literature. These interviews were published in a special issue of *Contemporary Literature* that was the first major critical source on Objectivist studies. In the absence of an extensive body of prose writings on poetics by Oppen, Dembo's interview with him is a crucial document.

Oppen had signed a contract in 1969 with Fulcrum Press in England for a *Collected Poems*, but during the next three years, the edition was delayed many times. Oppen despaired of ever seeing the book in print and became more and more exasperated with Fulcrum's editors, but the book finally appeared in 1972 and constitutes the first retrospective edition of his works. 1972 was also the year that saw the publication of *Seascape: Needle's Eye*, with Sumac Press of Fremont, Michigan. The latter book is concerned with the poet's relationship to the San Francisco Bay area, where he had grown up, but which he was now rediscovering through the optic of the '60s youth culture. He and Mary attended the Rolling Stones' Altamont concert in 1969—discussed in "Some San Francisco Poems"—which served as a lens through which Oppen's older Marxist sympathies were tested against New Left politics and New Age alternative lifestyles.

The late 1960s and early 1970s brought the Objectivists back into print—and into view. With the publication of Zukofsky's *"A"* and *All*, Reznikoff's *Collected Poems*, Lorine Niedecker's *Collected Poems*, and Carl Rakoski's *Amulet* and *Ere-Voice*, it became possible to see the Objectivists as a movement in ways that were never possible through their more ephemeral publications of the 1930s and 1940s. They formed a crucial link between the generation of Pound and Williams and the New American poets, such as Robert Creeley, Robert Duncan, and Charles Olson. And their work resonated with a younger generation of poets, such as Rachel Blau DuPlessis, Paul Auster, Ron Silliman, Barrett Watten, Sharon Olds, David Antin, David Bromige, John Taggart, Michael Palmer, and Charles Bernstein. What had seemed to critics to be a somewhat broken trajectory out of modernism was now being viewed as a specific continuity—an "Objectivist tradition," as Charles Altieri describes it—shaping several generations of postwar poets.[34] And there were European manifestations as well. During the early 1970s, having established important relationships with Charles Tomlinson, Christopher Middleton, and Jeremy Prynne in England and with Claude Royet-Journaud, Anne-Marie Albiach, and Serge Fauchereau in France, Oppen was invited to give a number of readings abroad. Oppen's notebooks and working papers are filled with comments on younger poets, and he and Mary attended many local readings around San Francisco.

Oppen's American *Collected Poems* was published by New Directions in 1975. The book reprinted all of his previous books—including *Discrete Series*—and included a final section of new poems, "The Myth of the Blaze," which at one point he considered using as his title for the entire volume. Writing to James Laughlin, the publisher of New Directions, Oppen mused on the meaning of "collected" by saying that the book "would give me what I badly need: a line drawn under the 45 years of work, a place to stand and from which to begin the step into what I hope . . . I would be able, finally, to do . . . during the next twenty years."[35] The book received an enthusiastic review by Hugh Kenner in *The New York Times Book Review* of October 19, and it was nominated for a National Book Award.

In 1975 George and Mary were invited by the mayor of Jerusalem to visit Israel. They stayed at Mishkenot Sha'ananim in Jerusalem, an artists' residence near the Old City, where they met a number of Israeli poets, their visit assisted by the presence of their old friend Shirley Kaufman, who was living in Israel.[36] Oppen had not been an observant Jew during his life, but he was excited and in trepidation over the trip. While in Jerusalem, he wrote "Disasters," a poem that testifies to his feelings of estrangement as a Jew who had seen the "disasters" of World War II and who, like other Jewish poets of his generation, found it difficult to write poetry after Auschwitz:

> *it is    dreary*
> *to descend*
>
> *and be a stranger* how
> shall we descend

who have become strangers in this wind that

rises like a gift
in the disorder[37]

    *Primitive*, from which this poem is taken, was published with Black Sparrow Press in 1978. It was the poet's last book, its title suggesting a return to what is basic and fundamental. Oppen was becoming increasingly confused and forgetful, and although it was not diagnosed as such, these were the signs of incipient Alzheimer's disease. His writing essentially stopped as of 1976 or '77 (his last dated effort, "The Poem," appears to have been written in 1980), although he continued to receive significant recognition for his contributions to literature. In 1980 the American Academy and Institute of Arts and Letters gave him an award "in recognition of his creative work in literature," and he was one of eight recipients of a one-time award from the National Endowment of the Arts for "extraordinary contributions to contemporary American literature over a lifetime of creative work." In 1981 the National Poetry Foundation published a special issue of the journal *Paideuma* devoted to Oppen's work, followed in 1982 by a full-length collection of biographical and critical materials, *George Oppen: Man and Poet*, edited by Burt Hatlen. In 1983, his seventy-fifth birthday was celebrated at an event sponsored by San Francisco State University.

    It is clear that throughout the late 1970s Oppen was aware of his changing mental capacities, although in public and private conversations those changes were somewhat masked by Mary's increasing tendency to complete his sentences. A review of his manuscript pages and late correspondence reveals increasing spelling errors and a deterioration of his already difficult penmanship. Although the symptoms of the disease had been evident since the mid-1970s, the more obvious signs of dementia emerged swiftly in the early 1980s. He was forced to leave his Polk Street home and entered the Idlewood Convalescent Home in Sunnyvale, California, where he died on July 7, 1984, at the age of seventy-six. On the walls of his Polk Street study, perhaps as a mnemonic against failing memory, Oppen had pasted a number of slips of paper, including one that reads: "I think I have written what I set out to say—I need not now turn to narrative. I have told not narrative but ourselves—no narrative but ourselves."[38]

# FORMS OF REFUSAL[39]

If in these introductory remarks I have stressed the role of the 1930s it is because George Oppen himself made it so central in his various interviews and worksheet notes. It is also a context liable to become obscured in more literary treatments of his work. Such treatments usually begin with his participation in the Objectivist movement, a loosely organized group of poets who came of literary age under the influence of Pound and Williams and who shared a belief in the values of the hard, spare artifact. Along with Charles Reznikoff, Louis Zukofsky, Lorine Niedecker, and Carl Rakosi, Oppen built on the lessons of Poundian Imagism, with its stress on the object clearly seen and directly presented. Zukofsky's essay "Sincerity and Objectification with Special Reference to the Work of Charles Reznikoff," published in the February 1931 "Objectivist" number of *Poetry*, would serve as a manifesto for the group, and work by Williams, Pound, and others would provide examples. Imagism projected the model of language divested of its "emotional slither," as Pound called it, returning to poetry the virtues of what Zukofsky called "sight, sound and intellection."

But Oppen was impatient with what he perceived as a gap between Imagist theory and the material world it proposed to present. "The weakness of Imagism," Oppen writes in a note, "[is that] a man writes of the moon rising over a pier who knows nothing about piers and is disregarding all that he knows about the moon."[40] This was his complaint about Pound in general, a poet Oppen much admired, but whose knowledge of history, he felt, came from books, not from experience. If Oppen's Objectivism can be broadly differentiated from Imagism, it is in the former's claim to experiential grounding of the poem: ". . . if Pound had walked into a factory a few times the absurdity of Douglas' theory of value, which Pound truculently repeats in the *Cantos* would have dawned on him—it sometimes pays to have a look . . . And to keep still till one has seen."[41] For all of Imagism's emphasis on the visual (Pound's "Petals on a wet, black bough"), Oppen felt it often overlooked the world on which it gazed. Objectivism served as a corrective to (not a repudiation of) Imagism's faith in the visual by linking the phenomenal object with an experiencing, language-using subject. Imagism was born in the era of (William) James and Whistler, Objectivism in the age of Whitehead and Wittgenstein.

As I have indicated, Oppen's more metaphysical concerns are often the result of material conditions—the exigencies of travel, work, and human intercourse—and the "little words" he loved so much are attached to a world as immediately encountered as a subway stop. We could extend this idea further by showing how it illustrates a dilemma at the heart of modernism, one between value and contingency. For Pound and Eliot, the problem of value in a world of fact was solved by containing quotidian reality in repetition, amassing cultural fragments toward an eternal dynastic edifice. Oppen chose to solve the problem not by adding more fragments to an already debased architecture but by refusing the building altogether—or at least by paying more attention to its building materials. We may see his gesture both as a refusal to speak in the face of political pressure, whether from the Stalinist censors or McCarthy's investigative committee, and as a refusal of the metaphysical lure of totality.

The context of refusal has a rich and varied history in American literature, one that begins with Puritanism and its fears of Antinomian rebellion. Poets from Edward Taylor and Anne Bradstreet through Emily Dickinson, Robert Creeley, and Jack Spicer have all been skeptical of the full, adequate word, preferring, as Emily Dickinson said, to "tell all the Truth but tell it slant." We may see George Oppen's poetics as emerging within this tradition, and we could identify three frames within which his refusal is embodied: the social, the epistemological, and the textual. As frames, these categories are by no means discrete but overlap and interpenetrate each other.

The social frame of Oppen's refusal is best viewed via the famous twenty-five-year hiatus between the writing of *Discrete Series* in 1934 and the beginning of *The Materials* in 1958 or '59. As Rachel Blau DuPlessis points out, this silence has exerted an unusual fascination among Oppen's readers. In a culture heavily committed to production, the idea of a writer who becomes silent seems heretical.[42] Hugh Kenner provided the most convenient explanation of Oppen's silence by observing that ". . . it took twenty-five years to write the next poem," a remark to which Oppen has given assent in various interviews.[43] However elegant, Kenner's formulation dehistoricizes Oppen's silence by sidestepping the challenges it was trying to meet during the politically charged 1930s. Oppen was not alone among writers on the left in rejecting Popular Front imperatives to write socially relevant work.[44] Rather than compose elegies for Lenin, as Zukofsky did, he channeled his labor in a different direction, joining the Communist Party, organizing tenant strikes, and working as an organizer. However much one may want to textualize his silence by seeing it as a lacuna in a long—a very long—poem, the facts of economic depression at home and the growth of Fascism abroad placed demands on his aesthetics that could not be resolved *through* aesthetics.

The second frame of refusal, the epistemological, refers to that odd merging of American pragmatism and European existentialism in Oppen's poetry. In both systems, knowledge is a relationship *between* rather than *of* things, a negotiation rather than an appropriation. For Whitehead, "the things experienced and the cognizant subject enter into the common world on equal terms."[45] There is, in other words, no privileged vantage, no natural standpoint, from which one may know either oneself or the entities that make up a phenomenal field. One finds oneself already in a world of intersecting particulars, no one of which may be isolated for purposes of scrutiny. Oppen is less interested in *what* is discovered than he is in the condition or mood in which things can be apprehended, in which things constellate a world. He often refers to Heidegger's discussion of boredom, in this regard ("the mood of boredom is the knowledge of what *is*, 'of the world, weather-swept'"), as a primary condition in which intentions have been removed and one becomes open to experience.[46] It is only within the profound indifference brought about by boredom that things and events can be revealed in their "thingness."

As forms of refusal, such ideas reject the authority of a reflective, Cartesian ego as well as a self-sufficient material world as the basis for ideas. In its place is the phenomenological realization that, as Oppen says, "consciousness exists and that it is consciousness of something . . . "[47] But how can we evaluate such consciousness if the object is indistinct (or more often, obscured by capital relations or ideology)? It is here that Zukofsky's idea of "sincerity" enters, the imperative that the poet attend to things in their unvarnished state, without subsuming their integrity to an instrumental rhetoric. Sincerity does not mean presenting a verbal mimesis of head gasket ("Image of the Engine") or saw ("Antique") but finding some linguistic approximation of cognitive acts engaged in apprehending such objects. Unlike Reznikoff or Williams, Oppen's aesthetics is decidedly nonvisual. He places his faith in parts of speech and speech acts rather than images, because it is only in its reduced, functional state that language may reveal its complicity in the production (rather than reflection) of reality. The image is a means to an end, not an end in itself. For Oppen, Imagism provided the test of sincerity—language free of what Zukofsky called "predatory intent"—out of which Objectivists could inaugurate a "test of truth"—language as participant in thought. This was a major distinction for poets who wanted their art to be more than a cultural repository or sign of authority. Oppen sought a poetry that, as he said, was a "method of thought," a place where questions could be asked and novelty investigated.

Directly linked to Oppen's social and epistemological frames of refusal is the form that silence takes in the poems. One could point to the way that any number of poems argue against totality by their use of partial elements:

> Thus
> hides the
> Parts——the prudery
> Of Frigidaire, of
> Soda-jerking——

Thus

Above the

Plane of lunch, of wives
Removes itself
(As soda-jerking from
the private act

Of
Cracking eggs);

big Business[48]

This brief early lyric suggests the ways that "big Business" hides its role in everyday life, much as Frigidaire hides its machinery behind white enamel or soda jerks hide the unseemly act of cracking eggs. One might add to this list Oppen's poem itself—the way that the conjunctive adverb, "Thus," implies an end that the poem refuses to deliver. By refusing to attach the word to any given agent ("Thus [one] Hides the / Parts," "Thus [big Business] Hides the / Parts" etc.) the speech act itself stands out as an empty sign of authority, removed from any relation to an agent. When "Thus" appears for the second time, it stands alone, unconnected to any syntactic element in lines that follow. One might reconfigure the sentence to read as follows: "big Business sits above the plane of lunch (lunch counters, wives who sit at lunch counters, the cracking of eggs for egg salad sandwiches, etc.), but this is not what Oppen says; he says, "Thus // Above the // Plane of lunch..." Prepositional phrases, parenthetical remarks, and noun phrases detached from predication atomize all linear sequence. The adverb does not follow from something, nor does it lead to something new. By refusing syntactic disclosure, Oppen participates in the very "prudery" he castigates, pointing *to* rhetorical power by emptying it of meaning. The lack of any terminal punctuation hints that this process is incomplete and that "big Business" continues well beyond the poem.

Not all of Oppen's poems are as conveniently "empty" as this one, but many participate in the same syntactic and rhetorical fragmentation. Such emphasis on the materiality of language is duplicated in his compositional method. He would build his poems vertically off the page, gluing revisions on top of previous text, or he would embed poems in the midst of other writings not connected to the poem.[49] In materializing the world as object (and the poem as "palimpsest" of other writings) Oppen calls attention not only to language as a structure but to the spaces that words are presumed to fill. He often figures this state by the image of glass, a substance that, depending on the light, may become translucent one moment, opaque the next. It is an image of modern society's insulation of itself within walls, even as it occasionally provides access to a world of vivid particulars. Glass functions as a frame for viewing poetry's refusal of presence, not for mirroring a more valid reality: "Closed car—closed in glass— / At the curb, / Unapplied and empty:"[50]

I began by speaking of a certain dilemma between value and contingency that modernist writers solved by linking the quotidian to mythic universals. Objectivism situated itself within that dilemma, regarding poetry as a productive force within the larger society—a "machine made out of words." But where Zukofsky attempted to return use-value to language by translating the terms of Marxian economics into repeated syllables and lines (in "A"-9) Oppen found value in the not said, in the incomplete phrase, in the bare noun. His silence was political in that it represented the inability of art to provide an adequate image of human suffering. His return to writing was political by representing the inability of communal forms to account for individual agency. What Pound recognized as Oppen's ability to manage a certain "void" may have included his ability to measure the distance between these two forms of refusal.

MICHAEL DAVIDSON

1. George Oppen, "The Anthropologist of Myself: A Selection From Working Papers," ed. Rachel Blau DuPlessis, *Sulfur* 26 (Spring 1990): 140. Hereafter abbreviated as S.
2. On Oppen's serial technique, see Alan Golding, "George Oppen's Serial Poems," *The Objectivist Nexus: Essays in Cultural Poetics*, ed. Rachel Blau DuPlessis and Peter Quartermain (Tuscaloosa: University of Alabama Press, 1999): 84–103. Hereafter abbreviated as ON.
3. Oppen is referring to Reznikoff's poem from *Jerusalem the Golden* (1934) in *The Complete Poems of Charles Reznikoff: Poems 1918–1936*, ed. Seamus Cooney, vol. 1 (Santa Barbara: Black Sparrow Press, 1976): 121. Oppen quotes this poem often, but he misremembers the actual words: "Among the heaps of brick and plaster lies / a girder, still itself among the rubbish."
4. George Oppen, "Memory at 'the Modern,'" *Elizabeth* VI (Oct., 1963): 1. See "Uncollected Published Poems," in *New Collected Poems* (New York: New Directions, 2001): 295. Hereafter abbreviated as NCP.
5. The line, "No other taste shall change this" is a riposte to Ezra Pound who, in Canto IV, tells the story of Guillem de Cabestan, a troubador who, according to Celtic legend, was the lover of Lady Seremonda. Cabestan is killed by her husband, who then serves her lover's heart to her. Pound's lines are as follows: "'It is Cabestan's heart in the dish? / 'No other taste shall change this.'" *The Cantos of Ezra Pound* (New York: New Directions, 1973): 13. On these lines and on Oppen's relationship to Pound, see Rachel Blau DuPlessis, "'The familiar / becomes extreme': George Oppen and Silence," *North Dakota Quarterly* 55.4 (Fall 1987): 18–36. See also her essay, "Objectivist Poetics and Political Vision: A Study of Oppen and Pound," *George Oppen: Man and Poet*, ed. Burton Hatlen (Orono, ME: National Poetry Foundation, 1981): 123–48. Hereafter abbreviated as GOMP.
6. NCP, 40.
7. In writing this brief biography, I have been aided by a year-by-year itinerary compiled by Rachel Blau DuPlessis and Mary Oppen and located in the George Oppen papers at the University of California, San Diego. I am also indebted to the following: Rachel Blau DuPlessis, "Introduction," *The Selected Letters of George Oppen* (Durham: Duke University Press, 1990), hereafter abbreviated as SL; Jeffrey Peterson, "George Oppen," *Dictionary of Literary Biography*, Vol. 165: American Poets Since World War II: Fourth Series (Detroit: Gale Research Inc., 1996): 188–206; Mary Oppen, *Meaning a Life: An Autobiography* (Santa Barbara: Black Sparrow Press, 1978), hereafter abbreviated as ML.
8. Some indication of his stepmother's abusive behavior can be seen in a note from Oppen's working papers, quoted in "'Meaning is to Be Here': A Selection from the Daybook," ed. Cynthia Anderson, *Conjunctions* 10 (1987): 193–94.
9. ML, 68.
10. SL, 365, n. 19.
11. S, 140.
12. *An "Objectivists" Anthology* offered Zukofsky a broad forum for presenting the Objectivist position through his essay "'Recencies' in Poetry" and by widening its participation from the core group (Oppen, Reznikoff, Zukofsky, Rakosi) to Basil Bunting, Mary Butts, Kenneth Rexroth, René Taupin, Robert McAlmon, and others. Louis Zukofsky, ed., *An "Objectivists" Anthology* (Paris: To Publishers, 1932). Reissued in 1975 by Folcroft Library Editions; reprinted in 1977 by Norwood Editions.
13. Quoted in Tom Sharp, "George Oppen, *Discrete Series*, 1929-1934," GOMP: 271.
14. ML: 132.
15. George Oppen, Interview with L.S. Dembo, *Contemporary Literature* 10.2 (Spring, 1969): 160. Hereafter abbreviated as CL. Oppen goes on to qualify this remark in his interview with Dembo by saying that it was "a little beyond the fact because there were differences of opinion on what should be included."
16. Quoted in ON: 4.
17. William Carlos Williams, "The New Poetical Economy," GOMP, 268.
18. NCP, 54.
19. NCP, 247. On Oppen's injuries during the war, see ML, 178.
20. On Oppen's war experiences, see David McAleavy, "The Oppens: Remarks Towards Biography," in *Ironwood* 26 (Fall, 1985): 309-18. Hereafter abbreviated as I.
21. They had every reason to be concerned. As Rachel Blau DuPlessis points out, the FBI had begun a dossier on Oppen as early as 1941, and their surveillance of his activities lasted until 1966 (SL, xv). According to Linda Oppen, the family was even watched while they lived in Mexico, and toward the end of their stay, they fled to Acapulco, fearing that the Mexican

government, in collusion with the FBI, would arrest them (personal communication).

22. Kevin Power, "An Interview with George and Mary Oppen," *Montemora* 4 (1978): 192.
23. David McAleavy, "The Oppens: Remarks Towards Biography" in I, 311. See also Rachel Blau DuPlessis in SL, xvii.
24. NCP, 52.
25. Eric Homberger, "Communists and Objectivists," ON, 107-25.
26. Ron Silliman calls the period from 1960 on, the "third or renaissance phase" of Objectivism, the second phase referring to the period of silence between 1940 and 1958, and the first referring to the inaugural moments of the 1930s. This third phrase also refers to the impact of Objectivism on a new generation of poets. See "Third Phase Objectivism" in *Paideuma* 10.1 (Spring 1981): 85-89.
27. George Oppen, "Three Poets," *Poetry* 100.5 (Aug. 1962): 329-32.
28. NCP, 193.
29. ML, 209.
30. NCP, 114.
31. NCP, 107.
32. NCP, 106.
33. The city's familiarity, through domestic associations, can be gleaned from a remark found among Oppen's papers: "I look in the broom closet, and I know I'm in San Francisco." Michael Davidson, "An Adequate Vision: A George Oppen Daybook," I, 11.
34. Charles Altieri, "The Objectivist Tradition," *Chicago Review* 30.3 (Winter 1979): 5-22.
35. SL, 283.
36. On the visit to Israel, see Shirley Kaufman, "The Obvious and the Hidden: Some Thoughts About 'Disasters,'" I, 152-58.
37. NCP, 267.
38. George Oppen papers, University of California, San Diego, folder 16, 19, 19. Hereafter abbreviated UCSD, followed by box and folder number. A selection of these fragments was edited by Stephen Cope and published in *Facture* 2 (2001): 1-10.
39. A version of this section, "Forms of Refusal: George Oppen's 'Distant Life,'" appeared in S, 127-34.
40. UCSD 16, 19, 4.
41. I, 17.
42. Rachel Blau DuPlessis, "'The familiar / becomes extreme': George Oppen and Silence," *North Dakota Quarterly* 55.4 (Fall 1987): 18.
43. See, for example, "A Conversation with George Oppen," ed. Charles Amirkhanian and David Gitin, *Ironwood* 5 (1975): 23-24; "Poetry and politics: A Conversation with George and Mary Oppen," eds. Burton Hatlen and Tom Mandel, GOMP: 24-25.
44. On Oppen's relationship to the left, see Eric Homberger, "George Oppen and the Culture of the American Left," GOMP: 181-93. See also Burton Hatlen and Tom Mandel, "Poetry and Politics: A Conversation with George and Mary Oppen," GOMP: 23-50.
45. Alfred North Whitehead, *Science and the Modern World* (New York: The Free Press, 1967): 89. See also Robert Von Hallberg's discussion of Whitehead's relationship to Objectivism in *Charles Olson: The Scholar's Art* (Cambridge: Harvard University Press, 1978): 82-87.
46. Quoted in CL, 169.
47. CL, 163
48. NCP, 7.
49. See Michael Davidson, "Palimtexts: George Oppen, Susan Howe, and the Material Text," *Ghostlier Demarcations: Modern Poetry and the Material Word* (Berkeley: University of California Press, 1997): 64-93.
50. NCP, 13.

# A Note on the Text

In selecting the poems for this edition, I have retained the integrity of George Oppen's individual volumes, making only slight changes as they occur in the 1975 *Collected Poems*. It is this latter volume that has served as my copy text, since it was the last full volume over which Oppen exerted complete control. The 1975 book collects the poet's five previous collections—*Discrete Series, The Materials, This in Which, Of Being Numerous, Seascape: Needle's Eye*—virtually unaltered from their separate editions. The one major change from the 1975 edition has been to return Oppen's first book, *Discrete Series*, to its original format of one poem per page and to include Ezra Pound's preface. As for poems published after 1975, I have added Oppen's last book, *Primitive* (1978), which, as my headnote to that volume indicates, involved some collaboration with his wife, Mary. Another small collection, *Alpine,* has not been included as a separate book, since most of its poems appear in other forms among Oppen's later poems.

References to the 1972 Fulcrum Press *Collected Poems* are contained in headnotes for individual books and poems. Earlier drafts of this volume were first sent to Cape and then to Oxford University Press in England but were not accepted by either press. The manuscript was then sent to Stuart Montgomery's Fulcrum Press, where a contract was offered and signed in March of 1969. It was originally to be called *The Collected Poems of George Oppen: 1929–1968* but was shortened to *Collected Poems of George Oppen* when it was published in 1972. The collection is substantially the same as the New Directions edition, although it omits several poems from each previous book. With *Seascape: Needle's Eye* (called "Of the Needle's Eye" in the Fulcrum edition), poems vary widely from those in New Directions. The dedication to Mary Oppen remains the same for both volumes. The epigraph to *Discrete Series* is taken from Ezra Pound's original preface to the 1934 volume: "We have ceased, I think, to believe that a nation's literature is anyone's personal property." In *The Materials*, Oppen omits the second epigraph by Yeats. The single epigraph to *This in Which* is "the third path, the arduous path of appearance" by Heidegger.

Besides *Primitive*, Oppen's uncollected poems have been added in two separate sections: "Uncollected Published Poems" and "Selected Unpublished Poems." The first section features poems that were printed in magazines or anthologies during Oppen's lifetime. Although individual poems may have been printed three or four times in separate venues, I have chosen the first publication to include here. Where significant variants occur in subsequent printings, they are discussed in the notes. David McAleavy has provided an excellent account of Oppen's publishing career in his "Bibliography of the Works of George Oppen" (*Paideuma* 10:1 [Spring 1981], 155–69), and I am indebted to his efforts in establishing my own selection. It is worth noting that, with the exception of early publications in *Poetry* or *An "Objectivists" Anthology* or Pound's *Active Anthology*, there are no magazine or anthology publications between the mid-1930s and the late 1950s, the period of Oppen's twenty-five period of "silence."

The second section, "Selected Unpublished Poems," provides a sampling from poems found among George Oppen's papers and correspondence. The Mandeville Department of Special Collections at the University of California, San Diego, where Oppen's papers are housed, lists 281 folders containing drafts of unpublished poems. Many of these drafts consist of stanzas or sections that eventually found their way into published poems, while many others appear to be fragments, trials, and false starts that Oppen never completed. My selection has been based on those poems for which there is evidence of sustained work or in which a title or marginal comment indicates some intention to include them in a given volume. A few of my selections have been chosen because they bear significantly on published poems, either by quoting lines that appear elsewhere or by extending themes or issues that emerge from his published volumes.

Choosing from among these various drafts and fragments is vexed on a number of fronts. For one thing, it is often difficult to determine when a poem is a poem and when it is a continuation of a prose remark on the same manuscript page. For every poem typed by itself on a single sheet of paper, there are dozens of others that appear in the midst of other kinds of writings, scribbles, lists, and prose jottings, heavily amended in pen and pencil. Oppen often began poems in the midst of writing letters or prose commentaries, retyping them in fair copy, and then revising them with marginal corrections. More often, Oppen would paste corrections directly on top of previous lines, creating a textual pile, often dozens of layers thick.[1]

These pages, what I have elsewhere called the poet's "daybook" and others have called "working papers," reflect Oppen's lifelong practice of jotting down observations, quotations, autobiographical notes, comments on poems, drafts of letters, laundry lists, responses to other poets.[2] These pages were written in numerous type fonts, pens, and markers, suggesting that he returned often to a given page to make additions over time. In many cases, these variegated sheets of paper would be bound together by pipe-stem cleaners, paper clips, or other connecting devices, in some attempt to collect scattered fragments of paper that had been lying around his desk. In some cases these folders or fascicles have a central theme. One such gathering includes drafts of letters and remarks on the sources to "Of Being Numerous"; another consists of drafts of the poem "Bahamas." Several bundles were intended to be used for public readings, his "offhand" interlinear commentary included among them. At the end of his life, and with the onset of Alzheimer's disease, he would paste or pin these sheets of paper to the walls of his study, creating a kind of mnemonic enclave of significant quotations, observations, and ruminations.[3] In the absence of more extensive prose writings, this "daybook" constitutes Oppen's major document of poetics, unsystematic yet rigorous in its interrogation of the work of poetry amid other intellectual and political concerns. As such, its integrity needs to be maintained and published as a separate document. Since that document will, I hope, be published one day, I have left many potentially interesting poetic fragments out of this volume so that they may be collected along with the surrounding prose.

I have discussed the interplay of these materials elsewhere, but I would here suggest that the editor, in a desire for an adequate copy text, must also respect the textual environment in which a poem appears. To present these poetic epigrams, fragments, and prose poems as elements of the *Collected Poems* might destroy a much more important textual imperative at work in the poet's life.[4] At the same time, since Oppen used these palimpsestic pages to draft poems that ultimately appeared in his various volumes, it is clear that he regarded the page as a site for many kinds of writing.

Since Oppen seldom dated his manuscripts, it is difficult to assign a specific period of composition for these unpublished poems. There is no evidence that Oppen composed poems between 1934 and 1958, nor are there notebooks or other documents among his papers from this period. Hence, it can be assumed that all of these unpublished poems were written between the late 1950s and the late 1970s. Wherever possible I have attempted to assign a provisional date based on internal evidence, letterhead, typeface, reference to other poems—and sheer conjecture. I have included in this section many poems selected by Rachel Blau DuPlessis in *Sulfur* magazine 25 (Fall 1989), which was the first posthumous selection of Oppen's work. I am indebted to DuPlessis for her work, although in some cases I have relied on a different manuscript or date of publication than hers. I have also reprinted a few of the poems that I published in *Ironwood* 26 (1985) as part of Oppen's "daybooks." Although both the *Sulfur* and *Ironwood* selections were technically "published," they occur in this unpublished section since they were edited after Oppen's death.

In both published and unpublished sections, I have made minor corrections of spelling and punctuation, while attempting to maintain the poet's idiosyncratic usages. Oppen often quoted from other sources in his poems, marking such appropriations by means of inverted commas or italics. Rather than change these to double quotation marks, I have retained his practice. The matter of spacing, particularly in poems drawn from manuscripts, is a more complex matter. Because Oppen often made corrections between lines or in the margins with directional arrows, it is difficult to know whether or not he intended to leave or delete a space. And in those cases where he made corrections by gluing a new line on top of an old one, the spacing intention is often difficult to gauge. I have based my spacing of his unpublished poems on the general pattern of lineation in a given poem and by observing where his indentations occur vis à vis the previous line.

As a poet of the page, Oppen used its margins and the spacing limitations of the typewriter to score his longer lines. When a line could not be extended into the right margin, he would often wrap and indent it as a second line. In some cases, this creates the possibility that the second line is, in fact, not a continuation but a new line. Since the published poem utilizes a different font from Oppen's typewriter, it becomes necessary to decide whether to create one long line or divide them as they appear on the typescript draft. Once again, I have made my decision to extend or divide a line based on whether the indentation seems consistent with other indented lines or if the previous line runs so near to the right margin that it was necessary to wrap it.

Textual notes have been designed to provide the general reader with an adequate background for understanding the poem and its place in Oppen's *oeuvre*. These notes do not by any means constitute a scholarly apparatus. Rather, they describe the provenance of a published poem, through previous magazine and anthology publications. In the case of an unpublished poem, I have indicated its location by box and folder number at the University of California, San Diego, Special Collections Department. Where relevant, I have described variants when they dramatically alter the meaning of the published poem or heighten semantic nuances otherwise obscured in the published version. I have paid special attention to marginal comments on typescripts that may help identify a given quotation or establish a date. The fact that "A Cultural Triumph" features a handwritten reference to an article in *Poetry* magazine by Hugh Kenner provides an interesting frame for Oppen's remarks about Marianne Moore; the literary texture of "Penobscot" (NCP, 123) is enlarged as a dialogue with William Carlos Williams when we learn that its original title was "So Much Depends Upon"; the title "Disasters," (NCP, 267) may suggest certain political views expressed in the poem, until we learn that its original title was "Senility," in which case the political is linked to the poet's awareness of his nascent Alzheimer's condition.

In addition to textual information, I have provided contextual details based on Oppen's biography, literary and cultural sources, political history, and other information. These notes are far from comprehensive and constitute a mixture of scholarly research and conjecture. I have been aided in this effort by Oppen's friends and family members, who have provided me with sources and allusions. Oppen was a "reader/writer," someone who wrote in response to passages in books or newspaper articles. The original source often became effaced in the process of writing the poem, yet its presence often animates the final product. I have tried to restore as many of those original textual sources as I can. Oppen's animus against obscurity and allusiveness notwithstanding, he often took great pains to decipher his sources in letters to friends and in interviews. These remarks have aided me in uncovering hard-to-locate sources, but there is much more for the literary archaeologist to uncover.

M. D.

1. Commenting on this procedure, Oppen has said: "What I do is I paste in the correction or change until the sheet becomes so thick it is no longer malleable. Then I copy it out straight. So that it may be two hundred versions, three hundred versions. I precisely lack Williams's sense of his own personal grace and the sureness of his own mannerisms. Nor do I want them." Quoted from "George and Mary Oppen: In Interview by Michel Englebert and Michael West," *American Poetry Review* 14:4 (July-Aug. 1985), 11.

2. Portions of Oppen's daybooks have been published in the following venues: "An Adequate Vision: A George Oppen Daybook," ed. Michael Davidson, *Ironwood* 26 (1985): 5-31; "'Meaning Is to Be Here': A Selection from the Daybook," ed. Cynthia Anderson, *Conjunctions* 10 (1987):186-208; "Selections from George Oppen's 'Daybook'," ed. Dennis Young, *The Iowa Review* 18:3 (Fall 1988): 1-17; "The Anthropologist of Myself; A Selection from Working Papers," ed. Rachel Blau DuPlessis, *Sulfur* 26 (1990): 135-64; *Selected Prose, Daybooks, and Papers* ed. Stephen Cope. (Berkeley: University of California Press, 2008).

3. MO discusses this habit in her interview with Dennis Young, *Iowa Review* 18:3 (Fall, 1988), 25.

4. Michael Davidson, "Palimtexts: George Oppen, Susan Howe and the Material Text," *Ghostlier Demarcations: Modern Poetry and the Material Word*. (Berkeley: University of California Press, 1997): 64-93.

# Acknowledgments

the myriad

lights have entered
us it is a music more powerful

than music

till other voices wake
us or we drown

The last poem in George Oppen's last book, *Primitive*, celebrates the sustaining value of other voices against J. Alfred Prufrock's solipsistic worry that those voices might "wake us, *and* we drown." Oppen was fortunate in his friends and family, and their loyalty to him inspired me in editing this edition of his *New Collected Poems*. I want first to thank Linda Oppen for her support of this project and for her help in identifying crucial historical and biographical details of her father's life. I also want to thank the staff of the Mandeville Department of Special Collections at the University of California, San Diego, where George Oppen's papers are stored. Bradley Westbrook, Steve Coy, Lynda Claassen, and others provided access to manuscripts, books, and documents and gave generously of their time in answering my questions. Brad Westbrook drew on his extensive knowledge of Oppen's archive to locate obscure lines and passages. Lynda Claassen, Director of Special Collections, allowed me to work directly with Oppen's fragile manuscript pages and provided me with photocopies and photographs of these pages.

The University of California, San Diego, provided much-needed research support. I was aided immeasurably by my research assistant and colleague, Stephen Cope, who helped locate and transcribe unpublished and uncollected poems. His conversations about Oppen's work and biography were a daily resource. A number of other friends and colleagues helped in compiling my notes. Thanks are extended to Burt Hatlen, Jerome Rothenberg, Michael Palmer, Edward Lee, Alex Mourelatos, Fred Randel, Louis Montrose, David McAleavy, Norman Finkelstein, Tony Edwards, David Crowne, Richard Cohen, and David Antin, all of whom helped me track down sources and references within the poems.

New Directions published the first American edition of Oppen's *Collected Poems* under the poet's supervision. This second version has been aided by the press's continued support of Oppen's poetry and of the Objectivist tendency in general. I am especially grateful to Barbara Epler of New Directions for encouraging me to take on this project and for her support throughout the process. My editor, Peter Glassgold, has been unstinting in his care for the minute details of overall design and copy. What coherence this volume exhibits is largely due to him. Thanks are also extended to Eliot Weinberger for his Preface and for his careful reading of the manuscript.

Finally, I want to acknowledge the extraordinary help provided by my two readers, Henry Weinfield and Rachel Blau DuPlessis. Both gave me excellent advice about organization and phrasing, and argued with me about my more extravagant (or insupportable) claims. The former's critical work on Oppen has been a vital resource, and I appreciated his comments on my use—and mis-use—of Oppen's philosophical terms. Rachel Blau DuPlessis's edition of Oppen's *Selected Letters* was an important model for my own editorial work, and her generous remarks, based on her long association with the poet, were invaluable.

Permission to quote from the papers of George Oppen has been granted by Linda Oppen, executor of the poet's estate, to whom thanks are extended. Finally, I want to thank Clayton Eshleman, editor of *Sulfur*, in whose pages a portion of the introduction appeared.

M. D.

A Morality Play:  Preface

A nature poet?
Yes.  Nature, _physis_.
What was the question?

Scope, a kind of redemption

The play          ! jagged
On the S          ico hills

A city street

Flats and stationery stores

Bars and restaurants

And the weight of the warehouses
Leads to the bay

Tamalpais in fog

Twain, Bret Harte -- humorous
For the Easterners

Place names                 local knowledge

Of        heavy hill

In the midst of nature the city
One is conscious of the farmlands also

And of grass and trees bent
Along the length of coast in the continual wind

It is not that one means to bring home
A moral to an audience

One is the selfish traveller
Happiest in foreign streets

The play begins with the world

A merciless logic

To produce a futile image

Image
Most loved, most loved, the great and the loved

In the less than thin air
Of a merciless process

The play begins with the world

We shall say it is impossible it should be either good or bad
If its colors are beautiful or if they are not beautiful
It is as remarkable in one case as the other

If it grows old and haggard we shall love it desperately

And if one steps into nothing
The fact is tremendous

Because we were taught to acknowledge only the middle,
The normal, we have lived beyond the public doctrine

We dreamed of girls

Original manuscript page of "A Morality Play: Preface"

# DISCRETE SERIES

## (1934)

# PREFACE

I. We have ceased, I think, to believe that a nation's literature is any-one's personal property.

Bad criticism emerges chiefly from reviewers so busy telling what they haven't found in a poem (or whatever) that they have omitted to notice what is.

The charge of obscurity has been raised at regular or irregular intervals since the stone age, though there is no living man who is not surprised on first learning that KEATS was considered "obscure." It takes a very elaborate reconstruction of England in Keats' time to erect even a shaky hypothesis regarding the probable fixations and ossifications of the then hired bureaucracy of Albemarle St., London West.

II. On the other hand the cry for originality is often set up by men who have never stopped to consider how much. I mean how great a variant from a known modality is needed by the new writer if his expression is to be coterminous with his content.

One distinguishes between young men who have seriously learned the processes of their elders, and who attempt to use extant tools well, or to invent new ones, and those who merely dress up in old clothes.

The need of "reform" depends entirely on the validity or invalidity of the modes in use. At certain times it is necessary to reform it altogether. At others the adequate variation from a known mode of writing is far less visible to the uninitiate.

I see the difference between the writing of Mr. Oppen and Dr.

Williams, I do not expect any great horde of readers to notice it. They will perhaps concentrate, or no, they will not concentrate, they will coagulate their rather gelatinous attention on the likeness.

I salute a serious craftsman, a sensibility which is not every man's sensibility and which has not been got out of any other man's books.

EZRA POUND

The knowledge not of sorrow, you were
        saying, but of boredom
Is——aside from reading speaking
        smoking——
Of what, Maude Blessingbourne it was,
        wished to know when, having risen,
"approached the window as if to see
        what really was going on";
And saw rain falling, in the distance
        more slowly,
The road clear from her past the window-
        glass——
Of the world, weather-swept, with which
        one shares the century.

**1**


White.   From the
Under arm of T

The red globe.

Up
Down.   Round
Shiny fixed
Alternatives

From the quiet

Stone floor . . .

2

    Thus
Hides the

Parts——the prudery
Of Frigidaire, of
Soda-jerking——

Thus

Above the

Plane of lunch, of wives
Removes itself
(As soda-jerking from
the private act

Of
Cracking eggs);

big-Business

The evening, water in a glass
Thru which our car runs on a higher road.

Over what has the air frozen?

Nothing can equal in polish and obscured
    origin that dark instrument
A car
    (Which.
Ease; the hand on the sword-hilt

Her ankles are watches
(Her arm-pits are causeways for water)

When she steps
She walks on a sphere

Walks on the carpet, dressing.
Brushing her hair

Her movement accustomed, abstracted,
Declares this morning a woman's
"My hair, scalp——"

1


The three wide
Funnels raked aft, and the masts slanted

        the
Deck-hand slung in a bosun's chair
Works on this 20th century chic and
        efficiency
Not evident at "The Sailor's Rest."

2

The lights, paving——
This important device
Of a race

Remains till morning.

       Burns
Against the wall.
He has chosen a place
With the usual considerations,
Without stating them.
Buildings.

The mast
Inaudibly soars; bole-like, tapering:
Sail flattens from it beneath the wind.
The limp water holds the boat's round
                              sides.  Sun
Slants dry light on the deck.
                    Beneath us glide
Rocks, sand, and unrimmed holes.

Closed car—closed in glass——
At the curb,
Unapplied and empty:
A thing among others
Over which clouds pass and the
                    alteration of lighting,
An overstatement
Hardly an exterior.
Moving in traffic
This thing is less strange——
Tho the face, still within it,
Between glasses—place, over which
                    time passes—a false light.

Who comes is occupied
Toward the chest (in the crowd moving
        opposite
Grasp of me)
                In firm overalls
The middle-aged man sliding
Levers in the steam-shovel cab,——
Lift (running cable) and swung, back
Remotely respond to the gesture before last
Of his arms fingers continually——
Turned with the cab. But if I (how goes
            it?)——
                    The asphalt edge
Loose on the plateau,
Horse's classic height cartless
See electric flash of streetcar,
 The fall is falling from electric burst.

PARTY ON SHIPBOARD


Wave in the round of the port-hole
Springs, passing,—arm waved,
Shrieks, unbalanced by the motion——
Like the sea incapable of contact
Save in incidents (the sea is not
    water)
Homogeneously automatic—a green capped
    white is momentarily a half mile
    out——
The shallow surface of the sea, this,
Numerously—the first drinks——
The sea is a constant weight
In its bed.  They pass, however, the sea
Freely tumultuous.

This land:
The hills, round under straw;
A house

With rigid trees

And flaunts
A family laundry,
And the glass of windows

Semaphoring chorus,
The width of the stage.   The usher from it:
Seats' curving rows two sides by distant
        phosphor.   And those 'filled';
Man and wife, removing gloves
Or overcoat.   Still faces already lunar.

The edge of the ocean,
The shore: here
Somebody's lawn,
By the water.

Tug against the river——
Motor turning, lights
In the fast water off the bow-wave:
Passes slowly.

She lies, hip high,
On a flat bed
While the after-
Sun passes.

Plant, I breathe——
                O Clearly,
Eyes legs arms hands fingers,
Simple legs in silk.

Civil war photo:
Grass near the lens;
Man in the field
In silk hat.   Daylight.
The cannon of that day
In our parks.

As I saw
There
Year ago——
If there's a bird
On the cobbles;
One I've not seen

Bolt
In the frame
Of the building——
A ship
Grounds
Her immense keel
Chips
A stone
Under fifteen feet
Of harbor
Water——
The fiber of this tree
Is live wood
Running into the
Branches and leaves
In the air.

From this distance thinking toward you,
Time is recession

Movement of no import
Not encountering you

Save the pulse cumulates a past
And your pulse separate doubly.

Town, a town,
But location
Over which the sun as it comes to it;
Which cools, houses and lamp-posts,
        during the night, with the roads——
Inhabited partly by those
Who have been born here,
Houses built——.  From a train one sees
        him in the morning, his morning;
Him in the afternoon, straightening——
People everywhere, time and the work
        pauseless:
One moves between reading and re-reading,
The shape is a moment.
From a crowd a white powdered face,
Eyes and mouth making three——
Awaited—locally—a date.

Near your eyes——
Love at the pelvis
Reaches the generic, gratuitous
            (Your eyes like snail-tracks)

Parallel emotions,
We slide in separate hard grooves
Bowstrings to bent loins,
            Self moving
Moon, mid-air.

Fragonard,
Your spiral women
By a fountain

'1732'

Your picture lasts thru us

       its air
Thick with succession of civilizations;
And the women.

No interval of manner
Your body in the sun.
You? A solid, this that the dress
                    insisted,
Your face unaccented, your mouth a mouth?
                    Practical knees:
It is you who truly
Excel the vegetable,
The fitting of grasses—more bare than
                    that.
Pointedly bent, your elbow on a car-edge
Incognito as summer
Among mechanics.

'O city ladies'
Your coats wrapped,
Your hips a possession

Your shoes arched
Your walk is sharp

Your breasts
        Pertain to lingerie

The fields are road-sides,
Rooms outlast you.

Bad times:
The cars pass
By the elevated posts
And the movie sign.
A man sells post-cards.

It brightens up into the branches
And against the same buildings

A morning:
His job is as regular.

On the water, solid——
The singleness of a toy——

A tug with two barges.

O what O what will
Bring us back to
Shore,
        the shore

Coiling a rope on the steel deck

## DRAWING

Not by growth
    But the
Paper, turned, contains
This entire volume

Deaths everywhere——
The world too short for trend is land——
    In the mouths,
        Rims

In this place, two geraniums
In your window-box
Are his life's eyes.

Written structure,
Shape of art,
More formal
Than a field would be
(existing in it)——
Her pleasure's
Looser;
'O—'

    'Tomorrow?'—

Successive
Happenings
(the telephone)

# THE MATERIALS

## *(1962)*

> We awake in the same moment to ourselves
> and to things.
>
> —Maritain

*misquotations
of*

> They fed their hearts on fantasies
> And their hearts have become savage.

*James*

*Maritian   AND   Pound*

*See note on back.*

ECLOGUE

The men talking
Near the room's center. They have said
More than they had intended.

Pinpointing in the uproar
Of the living room

An assault
On the quiet continent.

Beyond the window
Flesh and rock and hunger

Loose in the night sky
Hardened into soil

Tilting of itself to the sun once more, small
Vegetative leaves
And stems taking place

Outside—— O small ones,
To be born!

*[handwritten annotations: "center", "pinpoint", "2-3 stanza combo again", "enjambment lovely"]*

# IMAGE OF THE ENGINE

## 1

Likely as not a ruined head gasket
Spitting at every power stroke, if not a crank shaft
Bearing knocking at the roots of the thing like a pile-driver:
A machine involved with itself, a concentrated
Hot lump of a machine
Geared in the loose mechanics of the world with the valves
    jumping
And the heavy frenzy of the pistons. When the thing stops,
Is stopped, with the last slow cough
In the manifold, the flywheel blundering
Against compression, stopping, finally
Stopped, compression leaking
From the idle cylinders will one imagine
Then because he can imagine
That squeezed from the cooling steel
There hovers in that moment, wraith-like and like a plume
    of steam, an aftermath,
A still and quiet angel of knowledge and of comprehension.

## 2

Endlessly, endlessly,
The definition of mortality

The image of the engine

That stops.
We cannot live on that.
I know that no one would live out

Thirty years, fifty years if the world were ending
With his life.
The machine stares out,
Stares out
With all its eyes

Thru the glass
With the ripple in it, past the sill
Which is dusty——If there is someone
In the garden!
Outside, and so beautiful.


3

What ends
Is that.
        Even companionship
Ending.

'I want to ask if you remember
When we were happy! As tho all travels

Ended untold, all embarkations
Foundered.


4

On that water
Grey with morning
The gull will fold its wings
And sit. And with its two eyes
There as much as anything
Can watch a ship and all its hallways
And all companions sink.

5

*Also he has set the world*
*In their hearts.* From lumps, chunks,

We are locked out: like children, seeking love
At last among each other. With their first full strength
The young go search for it,

Native in the native air,
But even the beautiful bony children
Who arise in the morning have left behind
Them worn and squalid toys in the trash

Which is a grimy death of love. The lost
Glitter of the stores!
The streets of stores!
Crossed by the streets of stores
And every crevice of the city leaking
Rubble: concrete, conduit, pipe, a crumbling
Rubble of our roots

                    But they will find
In flood, storm, ultimate mishap:
Earth, water, the tremendous
Surface, the heart thundering
Absolute desire.

## POPULATION

Like a flat sea,
Here is where we are, the empty reaches
Empty of ourselves

Where dark, light, sound
Shatter the mind born
Alone to ocean

Save we are
A crowd, a population, those
Born, those not yet dead, the moment's

Populace, sea-borne and violent, finding
Incredibly under the sense the rough deck
Inhabited, and what it always was.

# RESORT

There's a volcano snow-capped in the air some twenty miles
      from here
In clear lit air,
There is a tree in leaf here——

In dream an old man walking,
An old man's rounded head
Abruptly mine

Self-involved, strange, alien,
The familiar flesh
Walking. I saw his neck, his cheek

And called, called:
Called several times.

## SOLUTION

The puzzle assembled
At last in the box lid showing a green
Hillside, a house,
A barn and man
And wife and children,
All of it polychrome,
Lucid, backed by the blue
Sky. The jigsaw of cracks
Crazes the landscape but there is no gap,
No actual edged hole
Nowhere the wooden texture of the table top
Glares out of scale in the picture,
Sordid as cellars, as bare foundations:
There is no piece missing. The puzzle is complete
Now in its red and green and brown.

## TRAVELOGUE

But no screen would show
The light, the volume
Of the moment, or our decisions

In the dugouts, roaring
Downstream with the mud and rainfalls to emergencies
Of village skills and the aboriginal flash

Of handsome paddles among the bright rocks
And channels of the savage country.

*is, a little bit Comedian*
*Showing / seeing / being*

# RETURN

*This Earth* the king said
Looking at the ground;
*This England.* But we drive
A Sunday paradise
Of parkway, trees flow into trees and the grass
Like water by the very asphalt crown
And summit of things
In the flow of traffic
The family cars, in the dim
Sound of the living
The noise of increase to which we owe
What we possess. We cannot reconcile ourselves.
No one is reconciled, tho we spring
From the ground together——

And we saw the seed,
The minuscule Sequoia seed
In the museum by the tremendous slab
Of the tree. And imagined the seed
In soil and the growth quickened
So that we saw the seed reach out, forcing
Earth thru itself into bark, wood, the green
Needles of a redwood until the tree
Stood in the room without soil——
How much of the earth's
Crust has lived
The seed's violence!
The shock is metaphysical.

For the wood weathers. Drift wood
And the foot print in the forest grow older.
This is not our time, not what we mean, it is a time

*[handwritten annotations: "This", "din", "Oh, wow – so Thomas Hardyish", "return / reversal → viewing what is natural as also violent → emergence as uprooting"]*

Passing, the curl at the cutwater,
The enormous prow
Outside in the weather. In that breeze,
The sense of that passage,
Is desertion,
Betrayal, that we are not innocent
Of loneliness as Pierrot, Pierrette chattering
Unaware tho we imagine nothing
Beyond the streets of the living——
A sap in the limbs. Mary,
Mary, we turn to the children
As they will turn to the children
Wanting so much to have created happiness
As if a stem to the leaves——

——we had camped in scrub,
A scrub of the past, the fringes of towns
Neither towns nor forest, nothing ours. And Linda five,
Maybe six when the mare grazing
In the meadow came to her.
'Horse,' she said, whispering
By the roadside
With the cars passing. Little girl welcomed,
Learning welcome. The rest is——

Whatever——whatever——remote
Mechanics, endurance,
The piers of the city
In the sea. Here are whole buildings
Razed, whole blocks
Of a city gone
Among old streets
And the old boroughs, ourselves
Among these streets where Petra beat
A washpan out her window gathering

A crowd like a rescue. Relief,
As they said it, The Relief. Petra
Decisive suddenly among her children
In those crumbling bedrooms, Petra,
Petra——. And how imagine it? or imagine
Coughlin in the streets,
Pelley and the Silver Shirts? The medieval sense seems
  innocent, the very
Ceremony of innocence that was drowned.
It was not. But how imagine it
Of streets boarded and vacant where no time will hatch
Now chairs and walls,
Floors, roofs, the joists and beams,
The woodwork, window sills
In sun in a great weight of brick.

*Now*

## FROM DISASTER

Ultimately the air
Is bare sunlight where must be found
The lyric valuables. From disaster

Shipwreck, whole families crawled
To the tenements, and there

Survived by what morality
Of hope

Which for the sons
Ends its metaphysic
In small lawns of home.

*lyric valuables*

# SARA IN HER FATHER'S ARMS

Cell by cell the baby made herself, the cells
Made cells. That is to say
The baby is made largely of milk. Lying in her father's arms,
    the little seed eyes
Moving, trying to see, smiling for us
To see, she will make a household
To her need of these rooms——Sara, little seed,
Little violent, diligent seed. Come let us look at the world
Glittering: this seed will speak,
Max, words! There will be no other words in the world
But those our children speak. What will she make of a world
Do you suppose, Max, of which she is made.

# BLOOD FROM THE STONE

## I

In the door,
Long legged, tall,
A weight of bone and flesh to her——
        Her eyes catch——
Carrying bundles. O!
Everything I am is
Us. Come home.

## II

The Thirties. And
A spectre

In every street,
In all inexplicable crowds, what they did then
Is still their lives.

As thirty in a group——
To Home Relief—the unemployed——
Within the city's intricacies
Are these lives. Belief?
What do we believe
To live with? Answer.
Not invent——just answer——all
That verse attempts.
That we can somehow add each to each other?

——Still our lives.

## III

And war.

More than we felt or saw.
There is a simple ego in a lyric,
A strange one in war.
To a body anything can happen,
Like a brick. Too obvious to say.
But all horror came from it.

      The need
To see past every rock, wall, forest
Among so many, carrying in its frightful danger
The brick body as in one's hands.
And rounding the corner of some wall
Into a farm yard——France——
The smell of wood-smoke from the kitchen;
An overwhelming sense of joy!
Stops everything. More still than the water trickling among
     the cobbles.
In boots. Steel helmet. Monstrous. Standing
Shut by the silent walls.

## IV

Fifty years
Sidereal time
Together, and among the others,
The bequeathed pavements, the inherited lit streets:
Among them we were lucky——strangest word.

The planet's
Time.

Blood from a stone, life
From a stone dead dam. Mother
Nature! because we find the others
Deserted like ourselves and therefore brothers. Yet

So we lived
And chose to live

These were our times.

## BIRTHPLACE: NEW ROCHELLE

Returning to that house
And the rounded rocks of childhood——They have lasted
    well.

A world of things.

An aging man,
The knuckles of my hand
So jointed! I am this?

                    The house
My father's once, and the ground. There is a color of his
        times
In the sun's light

A generation's mark.
It intervenes. My child,
Not now a child, our child
Not altogether lone in a lone universe that suffers time
Like stones in sun. For we do not.

Me! he says, hand on his chest.
Actually, his shirt.
               And there, perhaps,
The question.

Pioneers! But trailer people?
Wood box full of tools——
                  The most
American. A sort of
Shrinking
          in themselves. A
Less than adult: old.

A pocket knife,
A tool——
          And I
Here talking to the man?
             The sky

That dawned along the road
And all I've been
Is not myself? I think myself
Is what I've seen and not myself

A man marooned
No longer looks for ships, imagines
Anything on the horizon. On the beach
The ocean ends in water. Finds a dune
And on the beach sits near it. Two.
He finds himself by two.
             Or more.
'Incapable of contact

Save in incidents'
            And yet at night
Their weight is part of mine.
For we are all housed now, all in our apartments,
The world untended to, unwatched.
And there is nothing left out there
As night falls, but the rocks

*Song of Myself*
*Leaves of Grass.*

## STRANGER'S CHILD

Sparrow in the cobbled street,
Little sparrow round and sweet,
Chaucer's bird——

            or if a leaf
Sparkle among leaves, among the season's
Leaves——

       The sparrow's feet,
Feet of the sparrow's child touch
Naked rock.

## OZYMANDIAS

The five
Senses gone

To the one sense,
The sense of prominence

Produce an art
*De luxe.*

And down town
The absurd stone trimming of the building tops

Rectangular in dawn, the shopper's
Thin morning monument.

## DEBT

That 'part
Of consciousness
That works':

A virtue, then, a skill
Of benches and the shock

Of the press where an instant on the steel bed
The manufactured part——

New!
And imperfect. Not as perfect
As the die they made
Which was imperfect. Checked

To tolerance

Among the pin ups, notices, conversion charts,
And skills, so little said of it.

Some obfuscation
that occurred between
drafts

## PRODUCT

There is no beauty in New England like the boats. *place & yet*
Each itself, even the paint white
Dipping to each wave each time
At anchor, mast
And rigging tightly part of it
Fresh from the dry tools
And the dry New England hands.
The bow soars, finds the waves
The hull accepts. Once someone
Put a bowl afloat
And there for all to see, for all the children,
Even the New Englander
Was boatness. What I've seen
Is all I've found: myself.

## WORKMAN

Leaving the house each dawn I see the hawk
Flagrant over the driveway. In his claws
That dot, that comma
Is the broken animal: the dangling small beast knows
The burden that he is: he has touched
The hawk's drab feathers. But the carpenter's is a culture
Of fitting, of firm dimensions,
Of post and lintel. Quietly the roof lies
That the carpenter has finished. The sea birds circle
The beaches and cry in their own way,
The innumerable sea birds, their beaks and their wings
Over the beaches and the sea's glitter.

# THE UNDERTAKING IN NEW JERSEY

Beyond the Hudson's
Unimportant water lapping
In the dark against the city's shores
Are the small towns, remnants
Of forge and coal yard. The bird's voice in their streets
May not mean much: a bird the age of a child chirping
At curbs and curb gratings,
At barber shops and townsmen
Born of girls——
Of girls! Girls gave birth . . . But the interiors
Are the women's: curtained,
Lit, the fabric
To which the men return. Surely they imagine
Some task beyond the window glass
And the fabrics as if an eventual brother
In the fields were nourished by all this in country
Torn by the trucks where towns
And the flat boards of homes
Visibly move at sunrise and the trees
Carry quickly into daylight the excited birds.

*which is a vague way of describing*

## TOURIST EYE

*This activity, beginning in the midst of men . . .*

**1**

The lights that blaze and promise
Where are so many——What is offered

In the wall and nest of lights?
The land

Lacked center:
We must look to Lever Brothers

Based in a square block.
A thousand lives

Within that glass. What is the final meaning
Of extravagance? Why are the office

Buildings, storehouses of papers,
The centers of extravagance?

**2**

The solitary are obsessed.
Apartments furnish little solitude. Doors lock

On halls scarred
And painted. One might look everywhere

As tourists do, the halls and stairways
For something bequeathed

From time, some mark
In these most worn places

Where chance moves among the crowd
Unearned and separate

Among the crowd, the living, that other
Marvel among the mineral.

3

Rectangular, rearing
Black windows into daylight: the sound

Of a piano in the deep bulk tying
Generations to a Sunday that holds
As the building holds, only the adamant

Nothing that the child hopes,
Laboring a tune. From any window, the day

Flawless and without exterior
Without alternative. But to the tenant

The future is all chance, all future, and the present
All inanimate, or all herself.

4

The heart pounds
To be among them, the buildings,

The red buildings of Red Hook! In the currents of the harbor
The barn-red ferries on their curving courses
And the tides of Buttermilk Channel
Flow past the Brooklyn Hardware stores

And the homes
The aging homes
Of the workmen. This is a sense of order
And of threat. The essential city,
The necessary city
Among these harbor streets still visible.


5

Down-town
Swarms. Surely the oldest city,

It seems the oldest city in the world. Tho they are new in it.

                    But they too can become a fist
Having menace, the power of menace. After the headlines
          of last night

The streets appear unchanged,
Tho they are endangered,

By no means safe, the building tops
Unwarned and unwarnable.

## VULCAN

The householder issuing to the street
Is adrift a moment in that ice stiff
Exterior. 'Peninsula
Low lying in the bay
And wooded——' Native now
Are the welder and the welder's arc
In the subway's iron circuits:
We have not escaped each other,
Not in the forest, not here. The crippled girl hobbles
Painfully in the new depths
Of the subway, and painfully
We shift our eyes. The bare rails
And black walls contain
Labor before her birth, her twisted
Precarious birth and the men
Laborious, burly——She sits
Quiet, her eyes still. Slowly,
Deliberately she sees
An anchor's blunt fluke sink
Thru coins and coin machines,
The ancient iron and the voltage
In the iron beneath us in the child's deep
Harbors into harbor sand.

## FROM A PHOTOGRAPH

Her arms around me——child——
Around my head, hugging with her whole arms,
Whole arms as if I were a loved and native rock,
The apple in her hand——her apple and her father, and my
    nose pressed
Hugely to the collar of her winter coat. There in the photo-
    graph

it is the child who is the branch
We fall from, where would be bramble,
Brush, bramble in the young Winter
With its blowing snow she must have thought
Was ours to give to her.

Carrying their deckhands' bicycles
On deck beside the funnels,
Coming alongside in falling snow
As we had moved thru areas of falling snow
In shrunk northern curvatures
Of seas that are not East nor West——. Was it there you told
      of the man and the water of the Ganges,
The man with the domestic pitcher pouring the Ganges
Back? We imagined the Ganges
The warm belly of a girl swelled
Like India under the slacks. One might think himself Adam
Of the edges of the polar mist until the small black tugs of
      England
Came to fetch us in.

## TIME OF THE MISSILE

I remember a square of New York's Hudson River glinting
    between warehouses.
Difficult to approach the water below the pier
Swirling, covered with oil the ship at the pier
A steel wall: tons in the water,

Width.
The hand for holding,
Legs for walking,
The eye *sees!* It floods in on us from here to Jersey tangled
    in the grey bright air!

Become the realm of nations.

My love, my love,
We are endangered
Totally at last. Look
Anywhere to the sight's limit: space
Which is viviparous:

Place of the mind
And eye. Which can destroy us,
Re-arrange itself, assert
Its own stone chain reaction.

## THE MEN OF SHEEPSHEAD


Eric——we used to call him Eric——
And Charlie Weber: I knew them well,
Men of another century. And still at Sheepshead
If a man carries pliers
Or maul down these rambling piers he is a man who fetches
Power into the afternoon
                      Speaking of things

End-for-end, butted to each other,
Dove-tailed, tenoned, doweled——Who is not at home
Among these men? who make a home
Of half truth, rules of thumb
Of cam and lever and whose docks and piers
Extend into the sea so self-contained.

ANTIQUE

Against the glass
Towers, the elaborate
Horned handle of a saw
Dates back

Beyond small harbors
Facing Europe. Ship's hawser
On the iron bollard at the land's edge mooring
Continents of workmen

Where we built
Grand Central's hollow masonry, veined
In bolted rails in shabby
City limits daylight and the back yard

Homes. In which some show of flowers
And of kitchen water holds survival's
Thin, thin radiance.

## COASTAL STRIP

The land runs in a flat strip of jungle along the coast.
A dirt road, mile after mile, passable
To trucks in the dry season crossing
Powerful rivers. Occasionally a truck
Stalls in mid stream, the men
In the current, the bright stream of the river laboring
Over the wet wheels, the washed tires——
Alien tons thru the jungle. One comes suddenly
On villages, groups of palm houses, the people
At ease before the palm branch homes. They speak
Casually, if the truck stops, for this is the road.
      There are towns,
Cement and stucco cities on the banks of the rivers,
People crowding the streets
Carrying machetes in the city squares. And the girls
Packed in a boat load, beautiful in their dresses, swirling
Downstream in the bright water
Crossing to the town. It has all
Already happened, there can be no breath
Of wind in the trees, the houses
Of earth and of palm from the jungle. *The sea that made us*
      *islands* has events
Of gulf and Gulf Stream and the gales
That move across it——. We have come from some powerful
Surf to the West where that sea breaks
In salt on the continent.

## O WESTERN WIND

A world around her like a shadow
She moves a chair
Something is being made——
Prepared
Clear in front of her as open air

The space a woman makes and fills
After these years
I write again
Naturally, about your face

Beautiful and wide
Blue eyes
Across all my vision but the glint of flesh
Blue eyes
In the subway routes, in the small rains
The profiles.

again, seen
the individual
in [as the
collective/ numerous

## THE HILLS

That this is I,
Not mine, which wakes
To where the present
Sun pours in the present, to the air perhaps
Of love and of
Conviction.

        As to know
Who we shall be. I knew it then.
You getting in
The old car sat down close
So close I turned and saw your eyes a woman's
Eyes. The patent
Latches on the windows
And the long hills whoever else's
Also ours.

*He speaks of place with not just nostalgia on factuality / matter of factness but in a way that claims / stakes possession over it et simultaneously "unpossesses" it*

## THE SOURCE

If the city has roots, they are in filth.
It is a slum. Even the sidewalk
Rasps under the feet.

      ——In some black brick
      Tenement, a woman's body

Glows. The gleam; the unimaginable
Thin feet taper down
The instep naked to the wooden floor!

      Hidden and disguised
      ——and shy?

The city's
Secret warmth.

## CHARTRES

The bulk of it
In air

Is what they wanted. Compassion
Above the doors, the doorways

Mary the woman and the others
The lesser

Are dreams on the structure. But that a stone
Supports another

That the stones
Stand where the masons locked them

Above the farmland
Above the will

Because a hundred generations
Back of them and to another people

The world cried out above the mountain

What man could do,
And could not
And chance which has spared us
Choice, which has shielded us

As if a god. What is the name of that place
We have entered:
Despair? Ourselves?

That we can destroy ourselves
Now

Walking in the shelter,
The young and the old,
Of each other's backs and shoulders

Entering the country that is
Impenetrably ours.

## DAEDALUS: THE DIRGE

The boy accepted them;
His whole childhood in them, his difference
From the others. The wings
Gold,
Gold for credence,
Every feather of them. He believed more in the things
Than I, and less. Familiar as speech,
The family tongue. I remember
Now expedients, frauds, ridiculous
In the real withering sun blazing
Still. Who could have said
More, losing the boy anyway, anyway
In the bare field there old man, old potterer . . .

## PART OF THE FOREST

There are lovers who recall that
Moment of moonlight, lit
Instant——

But to be alone is to be lost
Altho the tree, the roots
Are there

       It is an oak: the word
Terrifying spoken to the oak——

The young men therefore are determined to be men.
Beer bottle and a closed door
Makes them men.

Or car.——Approach
A town to be negotiated
By the big machine

Slow, for a young
Woman, kids
In hand. She is

A family. Isn't tenderness, God knows,
This long boned girl——it is a kind of war,
       A tower

In the suburb.

Then the road again. The car's
Companion.

# SURVIVAL: INFANTRY

And the world changed.
There had been trees and people,
Sidewalks and roads

There were fish in the sea.

Where did all the rocks come from?
And the smell of explosives
Iron standing in mud
We crawled everywhere on the ground without seeing the
    earth again

We were ashamed of our half life and our misery: we saw
    that everything had died.

And the letters came. People who addressed us thru our
    lives
They left us gasping. And in tears
In the same mud in the terrible ground

*this muddling of prepositions
i v. interesting, also happens on pg
77*

## SQUALL

*Squall*

          coming about
When the squall knocked her
Flat on the water. When she came
Upright, her rig was gone
And her crew clinging to her. The water in her cabins,
Washing thru companionways and hatches
And the deep ribs
Had in that mid-passage
No kinship with any sea.

# CALIFORNIA

The headland towers over ocean
At Palos Verdes. Who shall say
How the Romantic stood in nature?
But I am sitting in an automobile
While Mary, lovely in a house dress, buys tomatoes from a
     road side stand.

And I look down at the Pacific, blue waves roughly small
     running at the base of land,
An area of ocean in the sun——
Out there is China. Somewhere out in air.
Tree by the stand
Moving in the wind that moves
Streaming with the waves of the Pacific going past.

              The beach: a child
Leaning on one elbow. She has swept an arm
To make a hollow and a mark around her in the sand,
A place swept smooth in one arm's claiming sweep beside
     the ocean,
Looking up the coast relaxed,
A Western child.
And all the air before her——what the wind brings past
In the bright simpleness and strangeness of the sands.

## SUNNYSIDE CHILD

As the builders
Planned, the city trees
Put leaves in summer air in lost
Streets above the subway. And in this

Achievement of the housed, this
Air, a child
Stands as a child,
Preoccupied

To find his generation, his contemporaries
Of the neighborhood whose atmosphere, whose sound
In his life's time no front door, no
Hardware ever again can close on.

# PEDESTRIAN

What generations could have dreamed
This grandchild of the shopping streets, her eyes

In the buyer's light, the store lights
Brighter than the lighthouses, brighter than moonrise

From the salt harbor so rich
So bright her city

In a soil of pavement, a mesh of wires where she walks
In the new winter among enormous buildings.

# TO MEMORY

*(From a poem by Buddhadeva Bose)*

## I

Who but the Goddess? All that is
Is yours. The causes, beginnings,
Are lost if you have lost them;
But from your eyelid's quiver

Flowers that are trampled spring
In their bloom before us, and a landscape deepens
Hill behind hill, and the branches
Bend in that sunlight——

The lute has no meaning,
Nor canvas, nor marble
Without you, nor the beaches

That shore the ocean,
The womb of our mother. Galaxies
Shine in that darkness——

O you who are darkness,
A core of our darkness, and illumination;
What your hands have let fall is lost to us.

**II**

Words, there are words!
But with your eyes
We see. And so we possess the earth.

Like an army of ants,
A multiple dry carcass
Of past selves

Moving
Thru a land dead behind us
Of deeds, dates, documents

Into the present of leaves.
What can our changes bring
To the flesh but the worm's old feast?

All that there is, is
Yours, and in the caves of your sleep
Lives in our permanent dawn.

## STILL LIFE

*(From a poem by Buddhadeva Bose)*

What *are* you, apple! There are men
Who, biting an apple, blind themselves to bowl, basket
Or whatever and in a strange spell feel themselves
Like you outdoors and make us wish
We too were in the sun and night alive with sap.

*surrealism*
*v/s*
*realism*

## LEVIATHAN

Truth also is the pursuit of it:
Like happiness, and it will not stand.

Even the verse begins to eat away
In the acid. Pursuit, pursuit;

A wind moves a little,
Moving in a circle, very cold.

How shall we say?
In ordinary discourse——

We must talk now. I am no longer sure of the words,
The clockwork of the world. What is inexplicable

Is the 'preponderance of objects.' The sky lights
Daily with that predominance

And we have become the present.

We must talk now. Fear
Is fear. But we abandon one another.

# THIS IN WHICH

# *(1965)*

'Wait a minute,' Randall said insistently. 'Are you trying to describe the creation of the world—the universe?'

'What else?'

'But—damn it, this is preposterous! I asked for an explanation of the things that have just happened to *us*.'

'I told you that you would not like the explanation.'

> ——Robert A. Heinlein,
> *The Unpleasant Profession of Jonathan Hoag*

'. . . the arduous path of appearance.'

> ——Martin Heidegger

# TECHNOLOGIES

Tho in a sort of summer the hard buds blossom
Into feminine profusion

The 'inch-sized
Heart,' the little core of oneself,
So inartistic,

The inelegant heart    → *that which is at the core but cannot hold*
Which cannot grasp
The world
And makes art

Is small

Like a small hawk    → *hawk/eagle → Dan Beachy Quick.*
Lighting disheveled on a window sill.

Like hawks we are at least not
Nowhere, and I would say
Where we are

Tho I distract
Windows that look out
On the business
Of the days

In streets
Without horizon, streets
And gardens
Of the feminine technologies
Of desire
And compassion which will clothe

Everyone, arriving
Out of uncivil
Air
Evil
As a hawk

From a hawk's
Nest as they say
The nest of such a bird

Must be, and continue
Therefore to talk about
Twig technologies

*That which will perish?*

*Construction*

# ARMIES OF THE PLAIN

## 1

'A zero, a nothing':
Assassin.

Not nothing. At nineteen
Crossing frontiers,

Rifleman of the suffering——
Irremediable suffering——of the not-great,

Hero and anti hero
Of our time

Despite all he has cost us
And he may have cost us very much

*The syntax misleads us into thinking that there will be a completion of the assertion of*

## 2

Ruby's day,
Bloomsday.

Ruby

Proud to have learned survival
On the harsh plains—— ——

Bloomsday.

A man
'Of the Jewish faith . . .'

'and it is so stupid . .
And I never use the term . .'

Whose people wrote
Greatly

Desperate the not great,
Like Oswald the not great

Locked
In combat.

The syntax grows even more
tangled

There is a portrait by Eakins
Of the Intellectual, a man
Who might be a school teacher
Shown with the utmost seriousness, a masculine drama
In the hardness of his black shoes, in the glitter
Of his eyeglasses and his firm stance——
How have we altered! As Charles said
Rowing on the lake
In the woods, 'if this were the country,
The nation, if these were the routes through it——'

How firm the man is
In that picture
Tho pedagogic.
This was his world. Grass
Grows to the water's edge
In these woods, the brown earth
Shows through the thinned grass
At the little landing places of vacation

Like deserted stations,
Small embarkation points: We are
Lost in the childish
Here, and we address
Only each other
In the flat bottomed lake boat
Of boards. It is a lake
In a bend of the parkway, the breeze
Moves among the primitive toys
Of vacation, the circle of the visible

The animal looked across
And saw my eyes . . . Vacation's interlude?

When the animal ran? What entered the mind
When dawn lit the iron locomotives,
The iron bridges at the edge of the city,

Underpinnings, bare structure,
The animal's bare eyes

In the woods . . .
'The relation of the sun and the earth

Is not nothing! The sea in the morning'
And the hills brightening, Loved

And not loved, the unbearable impact
Of conviction and the beds of the defeated,

Children waking in the beds of the defeated
As the day breaks on the million

Windows and the grimed sills
Of a ruined ethic

Bursting with ourselves, and the myths
Have been murderous,

Most murderous, stake
And faggot. Where can it end? Loved, Loved

And Hated,
Rococo boulevards

Backed by the Roman
Whose fluted pillars

Blossoming antique acanthus

Stand on other coasts
Lifting their tremendous cornices.

## PSALM

*Veritas sequitur . . .*


In the small beauty of the forest
The wild deer bedding down——
That they are there!

        Their eyes
Effortless, the soft lips
Nuzzle and the alien small teeth
Tear at the grass

        The roots of it
Dangle from their mouths
Scattering earth in the strange woods.
They who are there.

        Their paths
Nibbled thru the fields, the leaves that shade them
Hang in the distances
Of sun

        The small nouns
Crying faith
In this in which the wild deer
Startle, and stare out.

## THE *CITY OF KEANSBURG*

These are the small resorts
Of the small poor,
The low sandspits
And the honkytonks
On the far side
Of the becalmed bay. The pennant
Flies from the flagstaff
Of the excursion steamer
Which carried us
In its old cabins
Crossing the bay
Tho it is flimsily built
And fantastic, its three white decks
Towering now above the pier
That extends from the beach
Into water barely deep enough
Over the sand bottom.

# FIVE POEMS ABOUT POETRY

## 1

### THE GESTURE

The question is: how does one hold an apple
Who likes apples

And how does one handle
Filth? The question is

How does one hold something
In the mind which he intends

To grasp and how does the salesman
Hold a bauble he intends

To sell? The question is
When will there not be a hundred

Poets who mistake that gesture
For a style.

## 2

### THE LITTLE HOLE

The little hole in the eye
Williams called it, the little hole

Has exposed us naked
To the world

And will not close.

Blankly the world
Looks in

And we compose
Colors

And the sense

Of home
And there are those

In it so violent
And so alone

They cannot rest.


3

THAT LAND

Sing like a bird at the open
Sky, but no bird
Is a man——

Like the grip
Of the Roman hand
On his shoulder, the certainties

Of place
And of time

Held him, I think
With the pain and the casual horror
Of the iron and may have left
No hope of doubt

Whereas we have won doubt
From the iron itself

And hope in death. So that
If a man lived forever he would outlive
Hope. I imagine open sky

Over Gethsemane,
Surely it was this sky.


**4**

PAROUSIA

Impossible to doubt the world: it can be seen
And because it is irrevocable

It cannot be understood, and I believe that fact is lethal

And man may find his catastrophe,
His Millennium of obsession.

                       air moving,
a stone on a stone,
something balanced momentarily, in time might the lion

Lie down in the forest, less fierce
And solitary

Than the world, the walls
Of whose future may stand forever.

5

FROM VIRGIL

I, says the buzzard,
I——

Mind

Has evolved
Too long

If 'life is a search
For advantage.'

'At whose behest

Does the mind think?' Art
Also is not good

For us
Unless like the fool

Persisting
In his folly

It may rescue us
As only the true

Might rescue us, gathered
In the smallest corners

Of man's triumph. *Parve puer* . . . 'Begin,

O small boy,
To be born;

On whom his parents have not smiled

No god thinks worthy of his table,
No goddess of her bed'

## THE FORMS OF LOVE

Parked in the fields
All night
So many years ago,
We saw
A lake beside us
When the moon rose.
I remember

Leaving that ancient car
Together. I remember
Standing in the white grass
Beside it. We groped
Our way together
Downhill in the bright
Incredible light

Beginning to wonder
Whether it could be lake
Or fog
We saw, our heads
Ringing under the stars we walked
To where it would have wet our feet
Had it been water

## GUEST ROOM

There is in age

The risk that the mind
Reach

Into homelessness, 'nowhere to return.' In age
The maxims

Expose themselves, the happy endings
That justify a moral. But this?

This? the noise of wealth,

The clamor of wealth——tree
So often shaken——it is the voice

Of Hell.
The virtue of the mind

Is that emotion

Which causes
To see. Virtue . . .

Virtue . . . ? The great house
With its servants,

The great utensiled
House

Of air conditioners, safe harbor

In which the heart sinks, closes
Now like a fortress

In daylight, setting its weight
Against the bare blank paper.

◆　　◆

The purpose
Of their days.

And their nights?
Their evenings
And the candle light?

What could they mean by that?
Because the hard light dims

Outside, what ancient
Privilege? What gleaming
Mandate

From what past?

◆　　◆

If one has only his ability

To arrange
Matters, to exert force,

To open a window,
To shut it——

To cause to be arranged——

Death which is a question

Of an intestine
Or a sinus drip

Looms as the horror
Which will arrive

When one is most without defenses,

The unspeakable
Defeat

Toward which they live
Embattled and despairing;

It is the courage of the rich

Who are an *avant garde*

Near the limits of life——Like theirs

My abilities
Are ridiculous:

To go perhaps unarmed
And unarmored, to return

Now to the old questions——

      ◆   ◆

Of the dawn
Over Frisco
Lighting the large hills

And the very small coves
At their feet, and we
Perched in the dawn wind
Of that coast like leaves
Of the most recent weed——And yet the things

That happen! Signs,
Promises——we took it
As sign, as promise

Still for nothing wavered,
Nothing begged or was unreal, the thing
Happening, filling our eyesight
Out to the horizon——I remember the sky
And the moving sea.

## GIOVANNI'S *RAPE OF THE SABINE WOMEN*
## AT WILDENSTEIN'S

Showing the girl
On the shoulder of the warrior, calling

Behind her in the young body's triumph
With its despairing arms aloft

And the men violent,
being violent

In a strange village. The dust

Settles into village clarity
Among the villagers, a difficult

Song
Full of treason.

Sing?

To one's fellows?
To old men? in the villages,

The dwindling heritage
The heart will shrivel in

Sometime——But the statue!

Spiraling its drama
In the stair well

Of the gallery . . . Useless!
Useless! Thick witted,

*[handwritten marginalia: suddenly, in place / of a concrete / image place is / an abstract / noun]*

Thick carpeted, exhilarated by the stylish
Or the opulent, the blind and deaf. There was the child

The girl was:

Seeking like a child the eyes
Of the animals

To promise
Everything that matters, shelter

From the winds

The winds that lie
In the mind,
The ruinous winds

'Powerless to affect
The intensity of what is'——

'It has been good to us,'
However. The nights

At sea, and what
We sailed in, the large
Loose sphere of it

Visible, the force in it
Moving the little boat.

Only that it changes! Perhaps one is himself
Beyond the heart, the center of the thing

And cannot praise it

As he would want to, with the light in it, feeling the long
    helplessness
Of those who will remain in it

And the losses. If this is treason
To the artists, make the most of it; one needs such faith,

Such faith in it
In the whole thing, more than I,
Or they, have had in songs.

# A LANGUAGE OF NEW YORK

**1**

A city of the corporations

Glassed
In dreams

And images——

And the pure joy
Of the mineral fact

Tho it is impenetrable

As the world, if it is matter

Is impenetrable.

**2**

Unable to begin
At the beginning, the fortunate
Find everything already here. They are shoppers,
Choosers, judges . . . And here the brutal
Is without issue, a dead end.

                    They develop
Argument in order to speak, they become
unreal, unreal, life loses
solidity, loses extent, baseball's their game
because baseball is not a game

but an argument and difference of opinion
makes the horse races. They are ghosts that endanger

One's soul. There is change
In an air
That smells stale, they will come to the end
Of an era
First of all peoples
And one may honorably keep
His distance
If he can.


3

I cannot even now
Altogether disengage myself
From those men

With whom I stood in emplacements, in mess tents,
In hospitals and sheds and hid in the gullies
Of blasted roads in a ruined country,

Among them many men
More capable than I——

Muykut and a sergeant
Named Healy,
That lieutenant also——

How forget that? How talk
Distantly of 'the People'?

Who are the people? that they are

That force within the walls
Of cities

Wherein the cars
Of mechanics
And executives

Echo like history
Down walled avenues
In which one cannot speak.


4


Possible
To use
Words provided one treat them
As enemies.
Not enemies——Ghosts
Which have run mad
In the subways
And of course the institutions
And the banks. If one captures them
One by one proceeding

Carefully they will restore
I hope to meaning
And to sense.


5


Which act is
Violence

And no one makes do with a future
Of rapid travel with diminishing noise
Less jolting
And fewer drafts. They await

War, and the news
Is war
As always

That the juices may flow in them
And the juices lie.

Great things have happened
On the earth and given it history, armies
And the ragged hordes moving and the passions
Of that death

But who escapes
Death?

Whether or not there is war, whether he has
Or has not opinions, and not only warriors,
Not only heroes

And not only victims, and they may have come to the end
Of all that, and if they have
They may have come to the end of it.


6

There can be a brick
In a brick wall
The eye picks

So quiet of a Sunday.
Here is the brick, it was waiting
Here when you were born,

Mary-Anne


7


Strange that the youngest people I know
Like Mary-Anne live in the most ancient buildings

Scattered about the city
In the dark rooms
Of the past——and the immigrants,

The black
Rectangular buildings
Of the immigrants.

They are the children of the middle class.

'The pure products of America——'

Investing
The ancient buildings
Jostle each other

In the half-forgotten, that ponderous business,
This Chinese wall.

**8**

Whitman: 'April 19, 1864

The capital grows upon one in time, especially as they have got the great figure on top of it now, and you can see it very well. It is a great bronze figure, the Genius of Liberty I suppose. It looks wonderful toward sundown. I love to go and look at it. The sun when it is nearly down shines on the headpiece and it dazzles and glistens like a big star; it looks quite

curious . . .'

## EROS

*Show me also whether there is more to come than is past,*
*or the greater part has already gone by us.*—Second Esdras

'and you too, old man, so we have heard,
Once . . .'
An old man's head, bulging
And worn

Almost into death.

The head grows from within
And is eroded.

Yet they come here too, the old,
Among the visitors, suffering
The rain

Here above Paris——

To the plaque of the ten thousand
Last men of the Commune
Shot at that wall

In the cemetery of Père-Lachaise, and the grave
Of Largo Caballero and the monuments to the Resistance——

A devoutness

Toward the future
Recorded in this city
Which taught my generation

Art
And the great paved places
Of the cities.

Maze

And wealth
Of heavy ancestry and the foreign rooms

Of structures

Closed by their roofs
And complete, a culture

Mined
From the ground . . .

As tho the powerful gift
Of their presence
And the great squares void
Of their dead

Were the human tongue
That will speak.

*wow*

## BOY'S ROOM

A friend saw the rooms
Of Keats and Shelley
At the lake, and saw 'they were just
Boys' rooms' and was moved

By that. And indeed a poet's room
Is a boy's room
And I suppose that women know it.

Perhaps the unbeautiful banker
Is exciting to a woman, a man
Not a boy gasping
For breath over a girl's body.

## PENOBSCOT

Children of the early
Countryside

Talk on the back stoops
Of that locked room
Of their birth

Which they cannot remember

In these small stony worlds
In the ocean

Like a core
Of an antiquity

Non classic, anti-classic, not the ocean
But the flat
Water of the harbor
Touching the stone

They stood on——

I think we will not breach the world
These small worlds least
Of all with secret names

Or unexpected phrases——

Penobscot

Half deserted, has an air
Of northern age, the rocks and pines

And the inlets of the sea
Shining among the islands

And these innocent
People
In their carpentered

Homes, nailed
Against the weather——It is more primitive

Than I know
To live like this, to tinker
And to sleep

Near the birches
That shine in the moonlight

Distant
From the classic world——the north

Looks out from its rock
Bulging into the fields, wild flowers
Growing at its edges! It is a place its women

Love, which is the country's
Distinction——

The canoes in the forest
And the small prows of the fish boats
Off the coast in the dead of winter

That burns like a Tyger
In the night sky. One sees their homes and lawns,
The pale wood houses

And the pale green
Terraced lawns.
'It brightens up into the branches

*y space*

And against the buildings'
Early. That was earlier.

## SEATED MAN

The man is old and——
Out of scale

Sitting in the rank grass. The fact is
It is not his world. Tho it holds

The machine which has so long sustained him,
The plumbing, sidewalks, the roads

And the objects
He has owned and remembers.
He thinks of murders and torture

In the German cellars
And the resistance of heroes

Picturing the concrete walls.

*unusual usage that lends itself to more meaning(s)*

## STREET

Ah these are the poor,
These are the poor——

Bergen street.

Humiliation,
Hardship . . .

Nor are they very good to each other;
It is not that. I want

An end of poverty
As much as anyone

For the sake of intelligence,
'The conquest of existence'——

It has been said, and is true——

And this is real pain,
Moreover. It is terrible to see the children,

The righteous little girls;
So good, they expect to be so good . . .

## CARPENTER'S BOAT

The new wood as old as carpentry

Rounding the far buoy, wild
Steel fighting in the sea, carpenter,

Carpenter,
Carpenter and other things, the monstrous welded seams

Plunge and drip in the seas, carpenter,
Carpenter, how wild the planet is.

*beautiful*

## OF THIS ALL THINGS . . .

There are the feminine aspects,
The mode in which one lives
As tho the color of the air
Indoors
And not indoors

Only——. What distinction
I have is that I have lived
My adult life
With a beautiful woman, I have turned on the light
Sometimes, to see her

Sleeping——The girl who walked
Indian style——straight-toed——
With her blond hair
Thru the forests

Of Oregon
Has changed the aspect
Of things, everything is pierced
By her presence tho we have wanted
Not comforts

But vision
Whatever terrors
May have made us
Companion
To the earth, whatever terrors——

## THE PEOPLE, THE PEOPLE

For love we all go
To that mountain
Of human flesh
Which exists
And is incapable
Of love and which we saw
In the image
Of a woman——We said once
She was beautiful for she was
Suffering
And beautiful. She was more ambitious
Than we knew
Of wealth
And more ruthless——speaking
Still in that image——we will never be free
Again from the knowledge
Of that hatred
And that huge contempt. Will she not rot
Without us and die
In childbed leaving
Monstrous issue——

# BAHAMAS

Where are we,
Mary, where are we?
They screen us and themselves
With tree lined lanes

*shade / prevent from seeing / protect / prevent from entering*

And the gardens of hotels tho we have traveled
Into the affluent tropics. The harbors
Pierce all that. There are these islands

*→ anti-surreal here?*

Breaking the surface
Of the sea. They are the sandy peaks
Of hills in an ocean

Streaked green by their shoals. The fishermen
And the crews from Haiti
Tide their wooden boats out

In the harbors. Not even the guitarists
Singing the island songs
To the diners

Tell of the Haitian boats
Which bear their masts, the tall
Stripped trunks of trees

*Perhaps one of the most regular poems form-wise.*

(Perhaps a child
Barefoot on the ragged deck-load
Of coconuts and mats, leans

On the worn mast) across the miles
Of the Atlantic, and the blinding glitter
Of the sea.

## THE FOUNDER

Because he could not face
A whole day
From dawn

He lay late
As the privileged
Lie in bed.

Yet here as he planned
Is his village
Enduring

The astronomic light
That wakes a people
In the painful dawn.

*[handwritten annotations in margins:]*

*privileged    Lie*
*privileged    lie - in*
*privileged    (like in be*
*                   Strikce*

*The use of locators (place) the) are very interesting*

PRIMITIVE


A woman dreamed
In that *jacal*, a jungle hut, and awoke
Screaming in terror. The hut
Stands where the beach
Curves to a bay. Here the dug-out is hauled
Clear of the surf, and she awoke
In fear. Their possessions
Are in the hut and around it
On the clean ground under the trees: a length    *mid.*
   of palm trunk
Roughened by uses, a wash tub,
The delicate fish lines
His fingers know so well——
They were visible in the clear night. Here she awoke

Crying in nightmare
Of loss, calling her husband
And the baby woke also
Crying

*wow* .

ALPINE

We were hiding
Somewhere in the Alps
In a barn among animals. We knew
Our daughter should not know
We were there. It was cold
Was the point of the dream
And the snow was falling

Which must be an old dream of families
Dispersing into adulthood

And the will cowers
In the given

The outlaw winds
That move within barns

Intolerable breeze
A public music

Seeps thru the legendary walls
The cracked inner sides

The distinctions of what one does
And what is done to him blurrs

Bodies dream selves
For themselves

From the substance
Of the cold

Yet we move
Are moving

Are we not

Do we hear the heavy moving
Of the past in barns

*see Creely*

## RATIONALITY

there is no 'cure'
Of it, a reversal
Of some wrong decision——merely

The length of time that has passed
And the accumulation of knowledge.

To say again: the massive heart
Of the present, the presence
Of the machine tools

In the factories, and the young workman
Elated among the men
Is homesick

In that instant
Of the shock
Of the press

In which the manufactured part

New in its oil
On the steel bed is caught
In the obstinate links

Of cause, like the earth tilting
To its famous Summers——that 'part

of consciousness'. . .

## NIGHT SCENE

The drunken man
On an old pier
In the Hudson River,

Tightening his throat, thrust his chin
Forward and the light
Caught his raised face,
His eyes still blind with drink . . .

Said, to my wife
And to me——
He must have been saying

*Again*——

Good bye Momma,
Good bye Poppa

On an old pier.

# THE MAYAN GROUND

*. . . and whether they are beautiful or not there will be*
*no one to guard them in the days to come . .*

*We mourned the red cardinal birds and the jeweled*
    *ornaments*
*And the handful of precious stones in our fields . . .*

Poor savages
Of ghost and glitter. Merely rolling now

The tire leaves a mark
On the earth, a ridge in the ground

Crumbling at the edges
Which is terror, the unsightly

Silting sand of events——

Inside that shell, 'the speckled egg'
The poet wrote of that we try to break

Each day, the little grain,

Electron, beating
Without cause,

Dry grain, father

Of all our fathers
Hidden in the blazing shell

Of sunlight——. Savages,

Savages, there is no mystery about them,
Given the rest of it,

They who have evolved
In it, and no one to shield them

Therefore in the days to come, in the ruts
Of the road

Or the fields, or the thin
Air of the berserk mountains——. But the god!

They said,
Moving on the waters,

The breeze on the water, feathery
Serpent,

Wind on the surface,
On the shallows

And the count of the calendar had become confused.

They said they had lost account
Of the *unrolling of the universe*

And only the people

Stir in the mornings
Coming from the houses, and the black hair

Of the women at the pump

Against the dawn
Seems beautiful.

# QUOTATIONS

**1**

When I asked the very old man
In the Bahamas
How old the village was
He said,
'I found it.'

**2**

The infants and the animals
And the insects
'stare at the open'

And she said
*Therefore they are welcome.*

**3**

'. . . and her closets!
No real clothes——just astounding earrings
And perfumes and bright scarves and dress-up things——

She said she was "afraid," she said she was
"always afraid."'

**4**

And the child
We took on a trip
Said

'We're having the life of our times'

**5**

Someone has scrawled
Under an advertisement in the subway
Showing a brassy blond young woman.
With an elaborate head-dress:
'Cop's bitch.'

*(New York, 1962)*

Again, as Barzilai puts it, very
little editorializing, compared to
the amount of direct Reportage /
culling of facts, events, /quotes.

## RED HOOK: DECEMBER

We had not expected it, the whole street
Lit with the red, blue, green
And yellow of the Christmas lights
In the windows shining and blinking
Into distance down the cross streets.
The children are almost awed in the street
Putting out the trash paper
In the winking light. A man works
Patiently in his overcoat
With the little bulbs
Because the window is open
In December. The bells ring,

Ring electronically the New Year
Among the roofs
And one can be at peace
In this city on a shore
For the moment now
With wealth, the shining wealth.

# THE BICYCLES AND THE APEX

How we loved them
Once, these mechanisms;
We all did. Light
And miraculous,

They have gone stale, part
Of the platitude, the gadgets,
Part of the platitude
Of our discontent.

Van Gogh went hungry and what shoe salesman
Does not envy him now? Let us agree
Once and for all that neither the slums
Nor the tract houses

Represent the apex
Of the culture.
They are the barracks. Food

Produced, garbage disposed of,
Lotions sold, flat tires
Changed and tellers must handle money

Under supervision but it is a credit to no one
So that slums are made dangerous by the gangs
And suburbs by the John Birch Societies

But we loved them once,
The mechanisms. Light
And miraculous . . .

## THE OCCURRENCES

The simplest
Words say the grass blade
Hides the blaze
Of a sun
To throw a shadow
In which the bugs crawl
At the roots of the grass;

Father, father
Of fatherhood
Who haunts me, shivering
Man most naked
Of us all, O father

      watch
At the roots
Of the grass the creating
*Now*     that tremendous
plunge

# MONUMENT

Public silence indeed is nothing

So we confront the fact with stage craft
And the available poses

Of greatness,

One comes to the Norman chapel,
The Norman wall
Of the armed man
At the root of the thing,
Roughly armed,
The great sword, the great shield
And the helmet,
The horned helmet

On the mount
In the sea threatening
Its distances.

I was born to
A minor courage
And the harbor
We lived near, and the ungainliness
Of the merchants, my grandparents;

Of which I chose the harbor
And the sea

Which is a home and the homeless,
It is the sea,
Contrary of monuments
And illiberal.

## FLIGHT

Outside the porthole life, or what is
Not life streams in the air foils
Battering the wing tips, the houses
Small as in the skulls of birds, the frivolous ground

Of homes from which the force of motors
And the great riveted surfaces
Of the wings hold us, seated side by side
In fight, in the belly of force

Under the ceiling lights——the shabby bird
Of war, fear
And remoteness haunt it. We had made out
A highway, a city hall,

A park, but now the pastless ranches
Of the suburbs
Drift with the New World
Hills and the high regions

Which taken unaware
Resist, and the wings
Bend

In the open. Risk
And chance and event, pale
Ancestry beyond the portholes
Outside with the wings and the rivets.

# NIECE

The streets of San Francisco,
She said of herself, were my

Father and mother, speaking to the quiet guests
In the living room looking down the hills

To the bay. And we imagined her
Walking in the wooden past
Of the western city . . . her mother

Was not that city
But my elder sister. I remembered

The watchman at the beach
Telling us the war had ended—

That was the first world war
Half a century ago——my sister
Had a ribbon in her hair.

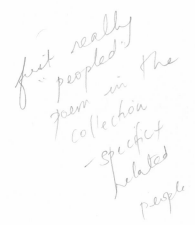

## THE ZULU GIRL

Her breasts
Naked, the soft
Small hollow in the flesh
Near the arm pit, the tendons
Presenting the gentle breasts
So boldly, tipped

With her intimate
Nerves

That touched, would touch her
Deeply——she stands
In the wild grasses.

# THE BUILDING OF THE SKYSCRAPER

The steel worker on the girder
Learned not to look down, and does his work
And there are words we have learned
Not to look at,
Not to look for substance
Below them. But we are on the verge
Of vertigo.

There are words that mean nothing
But there is something to mean.
Not a declaration which is truth
But a thing
Which is. It is the business of the poet
'To suffer the things of the world
And to speak them and himself out.'

O, the tree, growing from the sidewalk——
It has a little life, sprouting
Little green buds
Into the culture of the streets.
We look back
Three hundred years and see bare land.
And suffer vertigo.

## A NARRATIVE

### 1

I am the father of no country
And can lie.

But whether mendacity
Is really the best policy. And whether

One is not afraid
To lie.

### 2

And truth? O,
Truth!

Attack
On the innocent

If all we have
Is time.

### 3

The constant singing
Of the radios, and the art

Of colored lights
And the perfumist

Are also art. But here

Parallel lines do not meet
And the compass does not spin, this is the interval

In which they do not, and events
Emerge on the bow like an island, mussels

Clinging to its rocks from which kelp

Grows, grass
And the small trees

Above the tide line
And its lighthouse

Showing its whitewash in the daylight

In which things explain each other,
Not themselves.


4

An enclave
Filled with their own
Lives, they said, but they disperse

Into their jobs,
Their 'circles,' lose connection
With themselves . . . How shall they know

Themselves, bony
With age?
This is our home, the planets

Move in it
Or seem to,
It is our home. Wolves may hunt

With wolves, but we will lose
Humanity in the cities
And the suburbs, stores

And offices
In simple
Enterprise.


5


It is a place.
Nothing has entered it.
Nothing has left it.
People are born

From those who are there. How have I forgotten . .

How have we forgotten
That which is clear, we
Dwindle, but that I have forgotten
Tortures me.


6


I saw from the bus,
Walked in fact from the bus station to see again
The river and its rough machinery
On the sloping bank——I cannot know

Whether the weight of cause
Is in such a place as that, tho the depth of water
Pours and pours past Albany
From all its sources.


7

Serpent, Ouroboros
Whose tail is in his mouth: he is the root
Of evil,
This ring worm, the devil's
Doctrine the blind man
Knew. His mind
Is its own place;
He has no story. Digested

And digesting——Fool object,
Dingy medallion
In the gutter
Of Atlantic Avenue!
Let it alone! It is deadly.
What breath there is
In the rib cage we must draw
From the dimensions

Surrounding, whether or not we are lost
And choke on words.


8

But at night the park
She said, is horrible. And Bronk said
Perhaps the world
Is horror.

She did not understand. He meant
The waves or pellets
Are thrown from the process
Of the suns and like radar
Bounce where they strike. The eye
It happens
Registers
But it is dark.
It is the nature
Of the world:
It is as dark as radar.


9

      The lights
Shine, the fire
Glows in the fallacy
Of words. And one may cherish
Invention and the invented terms
We act on. But the park
Or the river at night
She said again
Is horrible.


10

Some of the young men
Have become aware of the Indian,
Perhaps because the young men move across the continent
Without wealth, moving one could say
On the bare ground. There one finds the Indian

Otherwise not found. Wood here and there
To make a village, a fish trap in a river,
The land pretty much as it was.

And because they also were a people in danger,
Because they feared also the thing might end,
I think of the Indian songs . . .
'There was no question what the old men were singing'
The anthropologist wrote,

Aware that the old men sang
On those prairies,
Return, the return of the sun.


**11**

River of our substance
Flowing
With the rest. River of the substance
Of the earth's curve, river of the substance
Of the sunrise, river of silt, of erosion, flowing
To no imaginable sea. But the mind rises

Into happiness, rising

Into what is there. I know of no other happiness
Nor have I ever witnessed it. . . . Islands
To the north

In polar mist
In the rather shallow sea——
Nothing more

But the sense
Of where we are

Who are most northerly. The marvel of the wave
Even here is its noise seething
In the world; I thought that even if there were nothing

The possibility of being would exist;
I thought I had encountered

Permanence; thought leaped on us in that sea
For in that sea we breathe the open
Miracle

Of place, and speak
If we would rescue
Love to the ice-lit

Upper World a substantial language
Of clarity, and of respect.

PRO NOBIS

I believe my apprenticeship
In that it was long was honorable
Tho I had hoped to arrive
At an actuality
In the mere number of us
And record now
That I did not.

Therefore pray for us
In the hour of our death indeed.

## TO C. T.

*(Written originally in a letter to Charles Tomlinson who, in his reply, suggested this division into lines of verse. The poem is, therefore, a collaboration.)*

One imagines himself
addressing his peers
I suppose. Surely
that might be the definition
of 'seriousness'? I would like,
as you see,
to convince
myself
that my pleasure in your response
is not
plain vanity
but the pleasure of being heard,
the pleasure
of companionship, which seems
more honorable.

Failure, worse failure, nothing seen
From prominence,
Too much seen in the ditch.

Those who will not look
Tho they feel on their skins
Are not pierced;

One cannot count them
Tho they are present.

It is entirely wild, wildest
Where there is traffic
And populace.

'Thought leaps on us' because we are here. That is the fact
        of the matter.
Soul-searchings, these prescriptions,

Are a medical faddism, an attempt to escape,
To lose oneself in the self.

The self is no mystery, the mystery is
That there is something for us to stand on.

We want to be here.

The act of being, the act of being
More than oneself.

# OF BEING NUMEROUS

## (1968)

## OF BEING NUMEROUS

### 1

There are things
We live among 'and to see them
Is to know ourselves'.

Occurrence, a part
Of an infinite series,

The sad marvels;

Of this was told
A tale of our wickedness.
It is not our wickedness.

'You remember that old town we went to, and we sat in the
ruined window, and we tried to imagine that we belonged to
those times——It is dead and it is not dead, and you cannot
imagine either its life or its death; the earth speaks and the sala-
mander speaks, the Spring comes and only obscures it——'

### 2

So spoke of the existence of things,
An unmanageable pantheon

Absolute, but they say
Arid.

A city of the corporations

Glassed
In dreams

And images——

And the pure joy
Of the mineral fact

Tho it is impenetrable

As the world, if it is matter,
Is impenetrable.


3


The emotions are engaged
Entering the city
As entering any city.

We are not coeval
With a locality
But we imagine others are,

We encounter them. Actually
A populace flows
Thru the city.

This is a language, therefore, of New York


4


For the people of that flow
Are new, the old

New to age as the young
To youth

And to their dwelling
For which the tarred roofs

And the stoops and doors——
A world of stoops——
Are petty alibi and satirical wit
Will not serve.


5


The great stone
Above the river
In the pylon of the bridge

'1875'

Frozen in the moonlight
In the frozen air over the footpath, consciousness

Which has nothing to gain, which awaits nothing,
Which loves itself


6


We are pressed, pressed on each other,
We will be told at once
Of anything that happens

And the discovery of fact bursts
In a paroxysm of emotion
Now as always. Crusoe

We say was
'Rescued'.
So we have chosen.


7

Obsessed, bewildered

By the shipwreck
Of the singular

We have chosen the meaning
Of being numerous.


8

*Amor fati*
The love of fate

For which the city alone
Is audience

Perhaps blasphemous.

Slowly over islands, destinies
Moving steadily pass
And change

In the thin sky
Over islands

Among days

Having only the force
Of days

Most simple
Most difficult

9

'Whether, as the intensity of seeing increases, one's distance
    from Them, the people, does not also increase'
I know, of course I know, I can enter no other place

Yet I am one of those who from nothing but man's way of
    thought and one of his dialects and what has happened
    to me
Have made poetry

To dream of that beach
For the sake of an instant in the eyes,

The absolute singular

The unearthly bonds
Of the singular

Which is the bright light of shipwreck

10

Or, in that light, New arts! Dithyrambic, audience-as-artists!
But I will listen to a man, I will listen to a man, and when I

speak I will speak, tho he will fail and I will fail. But I will
listen to him speak. The shuffling of a crowd is nothing——
well, nothing but the many that we are, but nothing.

Urban art, art of the cities, art of the young in the cities——
The isolated man is dead, his world around him exhausted

And he fails! He fails, that meditative man! And indeed they
cannot 'bear' it.


**11**

     it is *that* light
Seeps anywhere, a light for the times

In which the buildings
Stand on low ground, their pediments
Just above the harbor

Absolutely immobile,

Hollow, available, you could enter any building,
You could look from any window
One might wave to himself
From the top of the Empire State Building——


Speak


If you can


Speak

Phyllis——not neo-classic,
The girl's name is Phyllis——

Coming home from her first job
On the bus in the bare civic interior
Among those people, the small doors
Opening on the night at the curb
Her heart, she told me, suddenly tight with happiness——

So small a picture,
A spot of light on the curb, it cannot demean us

I too am in love down there with the streets
And the square slabs of pavement——

To talk of the house and the neighborhood and the docks

And it is not 'art'

**12**

'In these explanations it is presumed that an experiencing
subject is one occasion of a sensitive reaction to an actual
world.'

the rain falls
that had not been falling
and it is the same world

.      .      .

They made small objects
Of wood and the bones of fish
And of stone. They talked,

Families talked.
They gathered in council
And spoke, carrying objects.
They were credulous,
Their things shone in the forest.

They were patient
With the world.
This will never return, never,
Unless having reached their limits

They will begin over, that is,
Over and over

## 13

       unable to begin
At the beginning, the fortunate
Find everything already here. They are shoppers,
Choosers, judges; . . . And here the brutal
is without issue, a dead end.
                       They develop
Argument in order to speak, they become
unreal, unreal, life loses
solidity, loses extent, baseball's their game
because baseball is not a game
but an argument and difference of opinion
makes the horse races. They are ghosts that endanger

One's soul. There is change
In an air
That smells stale, they will come to the end
Of an era
First of all peoples
And one may honorably keep

His distance
If he can.

**14**

I cannot even now
Altogether disengage myself
From those men

With whom I stood in emplacements, in mess tents,
In hospitals and sheds and hid in the gullies
Of blasted roads in a ruined country,

Among them many men
More capable than I——

Muykut and a sergeant
Named Healy,
That lieutenant also——

How forget that? How talk
Distantly of 'The People'

Who are that force
Within the walls
Of cities

Wherein their cars

Echo like history
Down walled avenues
In which one cannot speak.

**15**

Chorus (androgynous): 'Find me
So that I will exist, find my navel
So that it will exist, find my nipples
So that they will exist, find every hair
Of my belly, I am good (or I am bad),
Find me.'


**16**

'. . . he who will not work shall not eat,
and only he who was troubled shall find rest,
and only he who descends into the nether world shall
    rescue his beloved,
and only he who unsheathes his knife shall be given
    Isaac again. He who will not work shall not eat . . .
but he who will work shall give birth to his own father.'


**17**

The roots of words
Dim in the subways

There is madness in the number
Of the living
'A state of matter'

There is nobody here but us chickens

Anti-ontology——

He wants to say
His life is real,
No one can say why

It is not easy to speak

A ferocious mumbling, in public
Of rootless speech

## 18

It is the air of atrocity,
An event as ordinary
As a President.

A plume of smoke, visible at a distance
In which people burn.

## 19

Now in the helicopters the casual will
Is atrocious

Insanity in high places,
If it is true we must do these things
We must cut our throats

The fly in the bottle

Insane, the insane fly

Which, over the city
Is the bright light of shipwreck

20

——They await

War, and the news
Is war

As always

That the juices may flow in them
Tho the juices lie.

Great things have happened
On the earth and given it history, armies
And the ragged hordes moving and the passions
Of that death. But who escapes
Death

Among these riders
Of the subway,

They know
By now as I know

Failure and the guilt
Of failure.
As in Hardy's poem of Christmas

We might half-hope to find the animals
In the sheds of a nation
Kneeling at midnight,

Farm animals,
Draft animals, beasts for slaughter
Because it would mean they have forgiven us,

Or which is the same thing,
That we do not altogether matter.


**21**


There can be a brick
In a brick wall
The eye picks

So quiet of a Sunday
Here is the brick, it was waiting
Here when you were born

Mary-Anne.


**22**


Clarity

In the sense of *transparence*,
I don't mean that much can be explained.

Clarity in the sense of silence.


**23**


'Half free
And half mad'
And the jet set is in.
The vocabularies of the forties
Gave way to the JetStream
And the media, the Mustang

And the deals
And the people will change again.

Under the soil
In the blind pressure
The lump,
Entity
Of substance
Changes also.

In two dozen rooms,
Two dozen apartments
After the party
The girls
Stare at the ceilings
Blindly as they are filled
And then they sleep.


24

In this nation
Which is in some sense
Our home. Covenant!

The covenant is
There shall be peoples.


25

Strange that the youngest people I know
Live in the oldest buildings

Scattered about the city
In the dark rooms
Of the past——and the immigrants,

The black
Rectangular buildings
Of the immigrants.

They are the children of the middle class.

'The pure products of America——'

Investing
The ancient buildings
Jostle each other

In the half-forgotten, that ponderous business.
This Chinese Wall.


**26**

They carry nativeness
To a conclusion
In suicide.

We want to defend
Limitation
And do not know how.

Stupid to say merely
That poets should not lead their lives
Among poets,

They have lost the metaphysical sense
Of the future, they feel themselves
The end of a chain

Of lives, single lives
And we know that lives
Are single

And cannot defend
The metaphysic
On which rest

The boundaries
Of our distances.
We want to say

'Common sense'
And cannot. We stand on

That denial
Of death that paved the cities,
Paved the cities

Generation
For generation and the pavement

Is filthy as the corridors
Of the police.

How shall one know a generation, a new generation?
Not by the dew on them! Where the earth is most torn
And the wounds untended and the voices confused,
There is the head of the moving column

Who if they cannot find
Their generation
Wither in the infirmaries

And the supply depots, supplying
Irrelevant objects.

Street lamps shine on the parked cars
Steadily in the clear night

It is true the great mineral silence
Vibrates, hums, a process
Completing itself

In which the windshield wipers
Of the cars are visible.

The power of the mind, the
Power and weight
Of the mind which
Is not enough, it is nothing
And does nothing

Against the natural world,
Behemoth, white whale, beast
They will say and less than beast,
The fatal rock

Which is the world——

O if the streets
Seem bright enough,
Fold within fold
Of residence . . .

Or see thru water
Clearly the pebbles
Of the beach
Thru the water, flowing
From the ripple, clear
As ever they have been

27

It is difficult now to speak of poetry——

about those who have recognized the range of choice or those who have lived within the life they were born to——. It is not precisely a question of profundity but a different order of experience. One would have to tell what happens in a life, what choices present themselves, what the world is for us, what happens in time, what thought is in the course of a life and therefore what art is, and the isolation of the actual

I would want to talk of rooms and of what they look out on and of basements, the rough walls bearing the marks of the forms, the old marks of wood in the concrete, such solitude as we know——

and the swept floors. Someone, a workman bearing about him, feeling about him that peculiar word like a dishonored fatherhood has swept this solitary floor, this profoundly hidden floor——such solitude as we know.

One must not come to feel that he has a thousand threads
      in his hands,
He must somehow see the one thing;
This is the level of art
There are other levels
But there is no other level of art


28

The light
Of the closed pages, tightly closed, packed against each other
Exposes the new day,

The narrow, frightening light
Before a sunrise.


**29**


My daughter, my daughter, what can I say
Of living?

I cannot judge it.

We seem caught
In reality together my lovely
Daughter,

I have a daughter
But no child

And it was not precisely
Happiness we promised
Ourselves;

We say happiness, happiness and are not
Satisfied.

Tho the house on the low land
Of the city

Catches the dawn light

I can tell myself, and I tell myself
Only what we all believe
True

And in the sudden vacuum
Of time . . .

... is it not
In fear the roots grip

Downward
And beget

The baffling hierarchies
Of father and child

As of leaves on their high
Thin twigs to shield us

From time, from open
Time

**30**

Behind their house, behind the back porch
Are the little woods.
She walks into them sometimes
And awaits the birds and the deer.

Looking up she sees the blue bright sky
Above the branches.
If one had been born here
How could one believe it?

**31**

Because the known and the unknown
Touch,

One witnesses——.
It is ennobling
If one thinks so.

If to know is noble

It is ennobling.

## 32

Only that it should be beautiful,
Only that it should be beautiful,

O, beautiful

Red green blue——the wet lips
Laughing

Or the curl of the white shell

And the beauty of women, the perfect tendons
Under the skin, the perfect life

That can twist in a flood
Of desire

Not truth but each other

The bright, bright skin, her hands wavering
In her incredible need

## 33

Which is ours, which is ourselves,
This is our jubilation

Exalted and as old as that truthfulness
Which illumines speech.


**34**


Like the wind in the trees and the bells
Of the procession——

How light the air is
And the earth,

Children and the grass
In the wind and the voices of men and women

To be carried about the sun forever

Among the beautiful particulars of the breezes
The papers blown about the sidewalks

' . . . . a Female Will to hide the most evident God
Under a covert . . .'

Surely infiniteness is the most evident thing in the world

Is it the courage of women
To assume every burden of blindness themselves

Intruders
Carrying life, the young women

Carrying life
Unaided in their arms

In the streets, weakened by too much need
Of too little

And life seeming to depend on women, burdened and
    desperate
As they are


35

. . . or define
Man beyond rescue
of the impoverished, solve
whole cities

before we can face
again
forests and prairies . . .


36

Tho the world
Is the obvious, the seen
And unforeseeable,
That which one cannot
Not see

*Women, creation*

Which the first eyes
Saw——

For us
Also each
Man or woman
Near is
Knowledge

Tho it may be of the noon's
Own vacuity

——and the mad, too, speak only of conspiracy
and people talking——

And if those paths
Of the mind
Cannot break

It is not the wild glare
Of the world even that one dies in.


**37**

'. . . approached the window as if to see . . .'

The boredom which disclosed
Everything——

I should have written, not the rain
Of a nineteenth century day, but the motes
In the air, the dust

Here still.

What have we argued about? what have we done?

Thickening the air?

Air so thick with myth the words *unlucky*
And *good luck*

Float in it . . .

To 'see' them?

No.

Or sees motes, an iron mesh, links

Of consequence

Still, at the mind's end
Relevant


**38**

You are the last
Who will know him
Nurse.

Not know him,
He is an old man,
A patient,
How could one know him?

You are the last
Who will see him
Or touch him,
Nurse.


**39**

Occurring 'neither for self
Nor for truth'

The sad marvels

In the least credible circumstance,
Storm or bombardment

Or the room of a very old man


**40**

Whitman: 'April 19, 1864

The capitol grows upon one in time, especially as they have got
the great figure on top of it now, and you can see it very well. It
is a great bronze figure, the Genius of Liberty I suppose. It looks
wonderful toward sundown. I love to go and look at it. The sun
when it is nearly down shines on the headpiece and it dazzles
and glistens like a big star: it looks quite


curious . . .'

## HISTORIC PUN

La petite vie, a young man called it later, it had been the
    last thing offered
In that way,
A way of behaving, a way of being in public
Which we lacked——

If there was doubt it was doubt of himself

Finding a force
In the cafés and bistros

Force of the familiar and familiars
The force of ease

They gather on the steps of Sacré-Coeur,
Great crowds, sitting on the steps
To watch the sunset and the lights——

I speak of tourists. But what we see is there

Find a word for ourselves
Or we will have nothing, neither faith nor will, the will

Touched by the dazzle——

Spring touches the Butte Chaumont,
Every morning the children appear
In the parks,
Paris is beautiful and ludicrous, the leaves of every tree in the
    city move in the wind
The girls have beautiful thighs, beautiful skirts, all simulate
    courage——

Semite: to find a way for myself.

# A KIND OF GARDEN: A POEM FOR MY SISTER

One may say courage
And one may say fear

And nobility
There are women

Radically alone in courage
And fear

Clear minded and blind

In the machines
And the abstractions and the power

Of their times as women can be blind

Untroubled by a leaf moving
In a garden

In mere breeze
Mere cause

But troubled as those are who arrive

Where games have been played
When all games have been won, last difficult garden

Brilliant in courage
Hard clash with the homely

To embellish such victories

Which in that garden
She sought for a friend

Offering gently

A brilliant kindness
Of the brilliant garden

## ROUTE

'the void eternally generative'
the Wen Fu of Lu Chi

**1**

Tell the beads of the chromosomes like a rosary,
Love in the genes, if it fails

We will produce no sane man again

I have seen too many young people become adults, young
       friends become old people, all that is not ours,

The sources
And the crude bone

          ——we say

*Took place*

Like the mass of the hills.

'The sun is a molten mass'. Therefore

Fall into oneself——?

Reality, blind eye
Which has taught us to stare——

Your elbow on a car-edge
Incognito as summer,

I wrote. Not you but a girl
At least

Clarity, clarity, surely clarity is the most beautiful
        thing in the world,
A limited, limiting clarity

I have not and never did have any motive of poetry
But to achieve clarity


2


Troubled that you are not, as they say,
Working——
I think we try rather to understand,
We try also to remain together

There is a force of clarity, it is
Of what is not autonomous in us,
We suffer a certain fear

Things alter, surrounded by a depth
And width

The unreality of our house in moonlight
Is that if the moonlight strikes it
It is truly there tho it is ours


3


Not to reduce the thing to nothing——

I might at the top of my ability stand at a window
and say, look out; out there is the world.

Not the desire for approval nor even for love——O,
that trap! From which escaped, barely——if it fails

We will produce no sane man again


4


Words cannot be wholly transparent. And that is the
    'heartlessness' of words.

Neither friends nor lovers are coeval . . .

as for a long time we have abandoned those in
    extremity and we find it unbearable that we should
    do so . . .

The sea anemone dreamed of something, filtering the sea
    water thru its body,

Nothing more real than boredom——dreamlessness, the
    experience of time, never felt by the new arrival,
    never at the doors, the thresholds, it is the native

Native in native time . . .

The purity of the materials, not theology, but to present
    the circumstances


5


   In Alsace, during the war, we found ourselves on the edge of
the Battle of the Bulge. The front was inactive, but we were
spread so thin that the situation was eerily precarious. We hard-

ly knew where the next squad was, and it was not in sight——a quiet and deserted hill in front of us. We dug in near a farm-house. Pierre Adam, tho he was a journeyman mason, lived with his wife and his children in that farmhouse.

During the occupation the Germans had declared Alsace a part of Greater Germany. Therefore they had drafted Alsatian men into the German army. Many men, learning in their own way that they were to be called, dug a hole. The word became a part of the language: *faire une trou*. Some men were in those holes as long as two and three years. It was necessary that some-one should know where those holes were; in winter it was impossible for a man to come out of his hole without leaving footprints in the snow. While snow was actually falling, howev-er, a friend could come to the hole with food and other help. Pierre, whom many people trusted, knew where some two dozen of those holes were.

The Germans became aware that men were going into hid-ing, and they began to make reprisals. If the man was young and unmarried, they killed his parents. If the man was married, they took his wife into Germany to the army brothels, it was said. They took the children into Germany, and it was not certain whether those children would remember where they came from. Pierre told me this story:

Men would come to Pierre and they would say: I am think-ing of making a hole. Pierre would say: yes. They would say then: but if I do they will kill my parents; or: they will take my wife and my children. Then Pierre would say, he told me: *if* you dig a hole, I will help you.

He knew, of course, what he was telling me. You must try to put yourself into those times. If one thought he knew anything, it was that a man should not join the Nazi army. Pierre himself learned, shortly before the Americans arrived, that he was about to be drafted. He and his wife discussed the children. They thought of tattooing the children's names and addresses on their chests so that perhaps they could be found after the war. But they thought that perhaps the tattooing would be cut out of the children . . . They did not, finally, have to make that decision, as it turned out. But what a conversation between a man and his wife——

There was an escape from that dilemma, as, in a way, there always is. Pierre told me of a man who, receiving the notification that he was to report to the German army, called a celebration and farewell at his home. Nothing was said at that party that was not jovial. They drank and sang. At the proper time, the host got his bicycle and waved goodbye. The house stood at the top of a hill and, still waving and calling farewells, he rode with great energy and as fast as he could down the hill, and, at the bottom, drove into a tree.

It must be hard to do. Probably easier in an automobile. There is, in an automobile, a considerable time during which you cannot change your mind. Riding a bicycle, since in those woods it is impossible that the tree should be a redwood, it must be necessary to continue aiming at the tree right up to the moment of impact. Undoubtedly difficult to do. And, of course, the children had no father. Thereafter.

6

Wars that are just? A simpler question: In the event,
will you or will you not want to kill a German. Because,
in the event, if you do not want to, you won't.

. . . and my wife reading letters she knew were two weeks

late and did not prove I was not dead while she read. Why did I play all that, what was I doing there?

We are brothers, we are brothers?——these things are composed of a moral substance only if they are untrue. If these things are true they are perfectly simple, perfectly impenetrable, those primary elements which can only be named.

A man will give his life for his friend provided he wants to.

In all probability a man will give his life for his child provided his child is an infant.

. . . One man could not understand me because I was saying simple things; it seemed to him that nothing was being said. I was saying: there is a mountain, there is a lake

A picture seen from within. The picture is unstable, a moving picture, unlimited drift. Still, the picture exists.

The circumstances:


7

And if at 80

He says what has been commonly said
It is for the sake of old times, a cozy game

He wishes to join again, an unreasonable speech
Out of context

8

Cars on the highway filled with speech,
People talk, they talk to each other;

Imagine a man in the ditch,
The wheels of the overturned wreck
Still spinning——

I don't mean he despairs, I mean if he does not
He sees in the manner of poetry


9

The cars run in a void of utensils
——the powerful tires——beyond
Happiness

Tough rubbery gear of invaders, of the descendents
Of invaders, I begin to be aware of a countryside
And the exposed weeds of a ditch

The context is history
Moving toward the light of the conscious

And beyond, culvert, blind curb, there are also names
For these things, language in the appalling fields

I remember my father as a younger man than I am now,
My mother was a tragic girl
Long ago, the autonomous figures are gone,
The context is the thousands of days

**10**

Not the symbol but the scene this pavement leads
To roadsides——the finite

Losing its purposes
Is estranged

All this is reportage.

If having come so far we shall have
Song

Let it be small enough.

Virgin
what was there to be thought

comes by the road


**11**

Tell the life of the mind, the mind creates the finite.

All punishes him. I stumble over these stories——
Progeny, the possibility of progeny, continuity

Or love that tempted him

He is punished by place, by scene, by all that holds
all he has found, this pavement, the silent symbols

Of it, the word it, never more powerful than in this
moment. Well, hardly an epiphany, but there the thing
is all the same

All this is reportage


**12**

To insist that what is true is good, no matter, no matter,
       a definition——?

That tree
      whose fruit . . .

The weight of air
Measured by the barometer in the parlor,
Time remains what it was

Oddly, oddly insistent

haunting the people in the automobiles,

shining on the sheetmetal,

open and present, unmarred by indifference,

wheeled traffic, indifference,
the hard edge of concrete continually crumbling

into gravel in the gravel of the shoulders,
Ditches of our own country

Whom shall I speak to


**13**

Department of Plants and Structures——obsolete, the old name
In this city, of the public works

Tho we meant to entangle ourselves in the roots of the world

An unexpected and forgotten spoor, all but indestructible
    shards

To owe nothing to fortune, to chance, nor by the power of
    his heart
Or her heart to have made these things sing
But the benevolence of the real

Tho there is no longer shelter in the earth, round helpless belly
Or hope among the pipes and broken works

'Substance itself which is the subject of all our planning'

And by this we are carried into the incalculable


**14**

There was no other guarantee

Ours aren't the only madmen tho they have burned thousands
of men and women alive, perhaps no madder than most

Strange to be here, strange for them also, insane and criminal,
who hasn't noticed that, strange to be man, we have come
rather far

We are at the beginning of a radical depopulation of the earth

Cataclysm . . . cataclysm of the plains, jungles, the cities

Something in the soil exposed between two oceans

As Cabeza de Vaca found a continent of spiritual despair
in campsites

His miracles among the Indians heralding cataclysm

Even Cortés greeted as revelation . . . No I'd not emigrate,
I'd not live in a ship's bar wherever we may be headed

These things at the limits of reason, nothing at the limits
of dream, the dream merely ends, by this we know it is the real

That we confront

᠈

# A THEOLOGICAL DEFINITION

A small room, the varnished floor
Making an L around the bed,

What is or is true as
Happiness  v/s  *catisfaction*

Windows opening on the sea,
The green painted railings of the balcony
Against the rock, the bushes and the sea running

*theological (see prev poem)*

# POWER, THE ENCHANTED WORLD

## 1

Streets, in a poor district——

*Crowded,*
We mean the rooms

Crowded, they come to stand
In vacant streets

Streets vacant of power

Therefore the irrational roots

We are concerned with the given

## 2

. . . *That come before the swallow dares.* . .

The winds of March

Black winds, the gritty winds, mere squalls and rags

There is a force we disregarded and which disregarded us

I'd wanted friends
Who talked of a public justice

Very simple people
I forget what we said

**3**

Now we do most of the killing
Having found a logic

Which is control
Of the world, 'we'               *cold war*
And Russia

What does it mean to object
Since it will happen?
It is possible, therefore it will happen
And the dead, this time, dead   → *reference to WW II*
                                   *ramifications?*

**4**

Power, which hides what it can

But within sight of the river

On a wall near a corner marked by the Marylyn Shoppe
And a branch bank

I saw scrawled in chalk the words, Put your hand on your
        heart

And elsewhere, in another hand,

Little Baby Ass

And it is those who find themselves in love with the world
Who suffer an anguish of mortality

5

Power ruptures at a thousand holes
Leaking the ancient air in,

The paraphernalia of a culture
On the gantries

And the grease of the engine itself
At the extremes of reality

Which was not what we wanted

The heart uselessly opens
To 3 words, which is too little

## BALLAD

Astrolabes and lexicons
Once in the great houses——

A poor lobsterman

Met by chance
On Swan's Island

Where he was born
We saw the old farmhouse

Propped and leaning on its hilltop
On that island
Where the ferry runs

A poor lobsterman

His teeth were bad

He drove us over that island
In an old car

A well-spoken man

Hardly real
As he knew in those rough fields

Lobster pots and their gear
Smelling of salt

The rocks outlived the classicists,
The rocks and the lobstermen's huts

And the sights of the island
The ledges in the rough sea seen from the road

And the harbor
And the post office

Difficult to know what one means
——to be serious and to know what one means——

An island
Has a public quality

His wife in the front seat

In a soft dress
Such as poor women wear

She took it that we came——
I don't know how to say, she said——

Not for anything we did, she said,
Mildly, 'from God'. She said

What I like more than anything
Is to visit other islands . . .

*multiplicity of similar experiences*

# SEASCAPE: NEEDLE'S EYE

*(1972)*

## FROM A PHRASE OF SIMONE WEIL'S
## AND SOME WORDS OF HEGEL'S


In          back         deep the jewel
The treasure
No          Liquid
Pride of the living life's liquid
Pride in the sandspit wind this ether this other this element all
It is I or I believe
We are the beaks of the ragged birds
Tune of the ragged bird's beaks
In the tune of the winds
Ob via          the obvious
Like a fire of straws
Aflame in the world or else poor people hide
Yourselves together          Place
Place where     desire
Lust of the eyes the pride of life and foremost of the storm's
Multitude moves the wave belly-lovely
Glass of the glass sea shadow of water
On the open water no other way
To come here the outer
Limit of the ego

## THE OCCURRENCES

Limited air      drafts
In the treasure house moving and the movements of the living
Things fall      something balanced      Move
With all one's force
Into the commonplace that pierces or erodes

The mind's structure but nothing
Incredible happens
It will have happened to that other
The survivor      The survivor
To him it happened

Rooted in basalt
Night hums like the telephone dial tone blue gauze
Of the forge flames the pulse
Of infant
Sorrows at the crux

Of the timbers
When the middle Kingdom
Warred with beasts Middle Things the elves the

Magic people in their world
Among the plant roots      hopes
Which are the hopes
Of small self interest called

Superstition chitinous
Toys of the children wings
Of the wasp

# ANIMULA

*animula blandula vagula*


Chance and chance and thereby starlit
All that was to be thought
Yes
Comes down the road     Air of the waterfronts     black air

Over the iron bollard     the doors cracked

In the starlight things the things continue
Narrative    their long instruction and the tide running
Strong as a tug's wake     shorelights'

Fractured dances across rough water a music
Who would believe it
Not quite one's own
With one always the     black verse     the turn and the turn

At the lens' focus     the crystal pool     innavigable

Torrent torment Eden's
Flooded valley          dramas

Of dredged waters
A wind blowing out

And out to sea          the late the salt times cling

In panicked
Spirals at the hull's side sea's streaks floating
Curved on the sea little pleasant soul wandering

Frightened

The small mid-ocean
Moon lights the winches

# WEST

Elephant, say, scraping its dry sides
In a narrow place as he passes says yes

This is true

So one knows?   and the ferns unfurling   leaves

In the wind

. . . sea         from which . .

'We address the future?   '

Unsure of the times
Unsure I can answer

To myself   We have been ignited
Blazing

In wrath we await

The rare poetic
Of veracity that huge art whose geometric
Light seems not its own in that most dense world West
        and East
Have denied have hated have wandered in   *precariousness*

*Like a new fire*

*Will burn out the roots*
One thinks of steep fields
Of brown grass
In the mountains it seems they lie

Aslant in the thin
Burning air and among clouds the sun
Passes boulders    grass blades    sky clad things

In nakedness
Inseparable                *the children will say*

*Our parents waited in the woods*                *precarious*

Transparent as the childhood of the world
Growing old    the seagulls sound like the voices of children
          wilder than children wildest of children the waves'
          riot
Brilliant as the world
Up side down         Not obstinate islands

This is the seaboard          New skilled fishermen
In the great bays and the narrow bights

# OF HOURS

' . . . as if a nail whose wide head
were time and space . . '

at the nail's point the hammer-blow
undiminished

Holes        pitfalls open
In the cop's accoutrement

Crevasse

The destitute metal

Jail metal

Impoverished       Intimate
As a Father did you know that

Old friend        old poet
Tho you'd walked

Familiar streets
And glittered with change the circle

Destroyed its content
Persists      the common

Place            image
The initial light        Walk on the walls

The walls of the fortress      the countryside
Broad in the night light the sap rises

Out of obscurities the sap rises
The sap not exhausted          Movement
Of the stone          Music
Of the tenement

Also is this lonely theme          Earth
My sister

Lonely sister my sister but why did I weep
Meeting that poet again what was that rage

Before Leger's art poster
In war time Paris perhaps art

Is one's mother and father          O rage
Of the exile          Fought ice

Fought shifting stones
Beyond the battlement

Crevasse          Fought

No man
But the fragments of metal
Tho there were men there were men          Fought
No man but the fragments of metal
Burying my dogtag with H
For Hebrew in the rubble of Alsace

*I must get out of here*

*Father*          he thinks          *father*

Disgrace of dying

Old friend        old poet
If you did not look

What is it you 'loved'
Twisting your voice        your walk

Wet roads

Hot sun on the hills

He walks twig-strewn streets
Of the rain

Walks homeward

Unteachable

## SONG, THE WINDS OF DOWNHILL

'out of poverty
to begin

again'   impoverished

of tone of pose that common
wealth

of parlance   Who
so poor the words

*would*   *with*   *and*   take on substantial

meaning   handholds   footholds

to dig in one's heels   sliding

hands and heels beyond the residential
lots   the plots   it is a poem

which may be sung
may well be sung

## SOME SAN FRANCISCO POEMS

**1**

*Moving over the hills, crossing the irrigation
canals perfect and profuse in the mountains the
streams of women and men walking under the high-
tension wires over the brown hills*

*in the multiple world of the fly's
multiple eye the songs they go to hear on
this occasion are no one's own*

*Needle's eye      needle's eye      but in the ravine
again and again on the massive spike the song
clangs*

*as the tremendous volume of the music takes
over obscured by their long hair they seem
to be mourning*

**2**

**A MORALITY PLAY: PREFACE**

Lying full length
On the bed in the white room

Turns her eyes to me

Again,

Naked . .

Never to forget her naked eyes

Beautiful and brave
Her naked eyes

Turn inward

Feminine light

The unimagined
Feminine light

Feminine ardor

Pierced and touched

Tho all say
Huddled among each other

'Love'

The play begins with the world

A city street
Leads to the bay

Tamalpais in cloud

Mist over farmlands

Local knowledge
In the heavy hills

The great loose waves move landward
Heavysided in the wind

Grass and trees bent
Along the length of coast in the continual wind

The ocean pounds in her mind
Not the harbor leading inward
To the back bay and the slow river
Recalling flimsy Western ranches
The beautiful hills shine outward

Sunrise          the raw fierce fire
Coming up past the sharp edge

And the hoof marks on the mountain

Shines in the white room

Provincial city
Not alien enough

To naked eyes

This city died young

You too will be shown this

You will see the young couples

Leaving again in rags


3

*So with artists.     How pleasurable*
*to imagine that, if only they gave*
*up their art, the children would be*
*healed,          would live.*
                    Irving Younger in *The Nation*

## 'AND THEIR WINTER AND NIGHT IN DISGUISE'

The sea and a crescent strip of beach
Show between the service station and a deserted shack

A creek drains thru the beach
Forming a ditch
There is a discarded super-market cart in the ditch
That beach is the edge of a nation

There is something like shouting along the highway
A California shouting
On the long fast highway over the California mountains

Point Pedro
Its distant life

It is impossible the world should be either good or bad
If its colors are beautiful or if they are not beautiful
If parts of it taste good or if no parts of it taste good
It is as remarkable in one case as the other
                                        As against this

We have suffered fear, we know something of fear
And of humiliation mounting to horror

The world above the edge of the foxhole belongs to the
        flying bullets, leaden superbeings
For the men grovelling in the foxhole danger, danger in
        being drawn to them

*These little dumps*
The poem is about them

Our hearts are twisted
In dead men's pride

Dead men crowd us
Lean over us

In the emplacements

The skull spins
Empty of subject

The hollow ego

Flinching from the war's huge air

Tho we are delivery boys and bartenders

We will choke on each other

Minds may crack

But not for what is discovered

Unless that everyone knew
And kept silent

Our minds are split
To seek the danger out

From among the miserable soldiers


**4**

ANNIVERSARY POEM

      'the picturesque
common lot'  the unwarranted light

Where everyone has been

The very ground of the path
And the litter grow ancient

A shovel's scratched edge
So like any other man's

We are troubled by incredulity
We are troubled by scratched things

Becoming familiar
Becoming extreme

Let grief
Be
So it be ours

Nor hide one's eyes
As tides drop along the beaches in the thin wash of
            breakers

And so desert each other

——lest there be nothing

            The Indian girl walking across the desert, the
sunfish under the boat

How shall we say how this happened, these stories, our
            stories

Scope, mere size, a kind of redemption

Exposed still and jagged on the San Francisco hills

Time and depth before us, paradise of the real, we
                    know what it is

To find now depth, not time, since we cannot, but depth

To come out safe,        to end well

We have begun to say good bye
To each other
And cannot say it


5

Combed thru the piers the wind
Moves in the clever city
Not in the doors but the hinges
Finds the secret of motion
As tho the hollow ships moved in their voices,    murmurs
Flaws
In the wind
Fear        fear
At the lumber mastheads
And fetched a message out of the sea again

Say angel        say powers

Obscurely  'things
And the self'

Prosody

Sings

In the stones

      to entrust
To a poetry of statement

At close quarters

A living mind
'and that one's own'

     what then         what spirit

Of the bent seas
         Archangel

of the tide
brimming

in the moon-streak

       comes in whose absence
earth crumbles


**6**

Silver as
The needle's eye

Of the horizon in the noise
Of their entrance row on row the waves
Move landward     conviction's

Net of branches
In the horde of events the sacred swarm avalanche
Masked in the sunset

Needle after needle more numerous than planets

Or the liquid waves
In the tide rips

We believe        we believe

Beyond the cable car streets
And the picture window

Lives the glittering crumbling night
Of obstructions and the stark structures

That carry wires over the mountain
One writes in the presence of something
Moving close to fear
I dare pity no one
Let the rafters pity
The air in the room
Under the rafters
Pity
In the continual sound
Are chords
Not yet struck
Which will be struck
Nevertheless yes


7

O withering seas
Of the doorstep and local winds unveil

The face of art

*Carpenter, plunge and drip in the sea*    Art's face
We know that face

More blinding than the sea    a haunted house    a limited

Consensus unwinding

Its powers
Toward the thread's end

In the record of great blows    shocks
Ravishment    devastation    the wood splintered

The keyboard gone in the rank grass swept her hand
Over the strings and the thing rang out

Over the rocks and the ocean
Not my poem    Mr Steinway's

Poem    Not mine    A 'marvelous' object
Is not the marvel of things

          twisting the new
Mouth    forcing the new
Tongue    But it rang


8


THE TASTE


Old ships are preserved
For their queer silence of obedient seas
Their cutwaters floating in the still water
With their cozy black iron work

And Swedish seamen dead     the cabins
Hold the spaces of their deaths
And the hammered nails of necessity
Carried thru the oceans
Where the moon rises grandly
In the grandeur of cause
We have a taste for bedrock
Beneath this spectacle
To gawk at
Something is wrong with the antiques, a black fluid
Has covered them, a black splintering
Under the eyes of young wives
People talk wildly, we are beginning to talk wildly, the wind
At every summit
Our overcoats trip us
Running for the bus
Our arms stretched out
In a wind from what were sand dunes


## 9


THE IMPOSSIBLE POEM


Climbing the peak of Tamalpais the loose
Gravel underfoot

And the city shining with the tremendous wrinkles
In the hills and the winding of the bay
Behind it, it faces the bent ocean

Streetcars
Rocked thru the city and the winds
Combed their clumsy sides

In clumsy times

Sierras withering
Behind the storefronts

And sanity the roadside weed
Dreams of sports and sportsmanship

In the lucid towns paralyzed
Under the truck tires
Shall we relinquish

Sanity to redeem
Fragments and fragmentary
Histories in the towns and the temperate streets
Too shallow still to drown in or to mourn
The courageous and precarious children


10

BUT SO AS BY FIRE

The darkness of trees
Guards this life
Of the thin ground
That covers the rock ledge

Among the lanes and magic
Of the Eastern woods

The beauty of silence
And broken boughs

And the homes of small animals

The green leaves
Of young plants
Above the dark green moss
In the sweet smell of rot

The pools and the trickle of freshwater

First life,     rotting life
Hidden starry life it is not yet

A mirror
Like our lives

We have gone
As far as is possible

Whose lives reflect light
Like mirrors

One had not thought
To be afraid

Not of shadow but of light

Summon one's powers

# EXODUS

Miracle of the children       the brilliant
Children      the word
Liquid as woodlands      Children?

When she was a child I read Exodus
To my daughter     'The children of Israel. . .'

Pillar of fire
Pillar of cloud

We stared at the end
Into each other's eyes      Where
She said hushed

Were the adults    We dreamed to each other
Miracle of the children
The brilliant children      Miracle

Of their brilliance      Miracle
of

# MYTH OF THE BLAZE

## *(1972-1975)*

LATITUDE, LONGITUDE


      climbed from the road and found
over the flowers at the mountain's
rough top a bee yellow
and heavy as

      pollen in the mountainous
air thin legs crookedly
a-dangle if we could

find all
the gale's evidence what message
is there for us in these
glassy bottles the Encyclopedist

was wrong was wrong many things
too foolish
to sing
may be said this matter-
of-fact defines

poetry

## THE SPEECH AT SOLI

what do you want
to tell while the world

speaks nights or some nights
sleepless

fearful remembering
myself in these towns or by car

thru these towns       unconscionable

adolescent young girls fall into wells

says a letter

bringing to birth

in the green storm

anger.     anger,
and the light of the self small
blazing sun of the farms——          return

the return of the sun there are actors'

faces of the highways the theatre
greets itself and reverberates the spirit
goes down goes under
stationary
valves of ditches the chartered
rivers threats in stones
enemies in sidewalks and when the stars rise
reverse ourselves regions of the mind

alter
mad kings

gone raving

war in incoherent
sunlight it will not

cohere it will N O T that
other

desertion
of the total we discover

Friday's footprint is it as the sun moves

beyond the blunt
towns of the coast        fishermen's

tumbled tumbling headlands the needle silver
water, and tells the public time

# THE BOOK OF JOB AND A DRAFT OF A POEM
## TO PRAISE THE PATHS OF THE LIVING

*in memory of Mickey Schwerner*


image    the images    the great games therefore the locked

the half-lit jailwinds

in the veins the lynch gangs

simulate blows    bruise        the bones
breaking      *age*

*of the world's deeds this is the young age*        age

of the sea's surf    image    image

of the world its least rags
stream among the planets    Our
lady of poverty the lever the fulcrum
the cam and the ant
hath her anger and the emmet
his choler the exposed
belly of the land
under the sky
at night and the windy pines unleash
the morning's force what is the form
to say it there is something
to name Goodman    Schwerner    Chaney
who were beaten not we
who were beaten        children
not our
children        ancestral

children rose in the dark
to their work there grows
there builds there is written
a vividness     there is     rawness
like a new sun the flames
tremendous the sun
itself ourselves ourselves
go with us *disorder*

*so great the tumult wave*

*upon wave* this traverse

this desert                    extravagant
*island of light*

◆        ◆

the long road
going north

on the cliffs          small
and numerous

the windows

look out on the sea's simulacra
of self-evidence          meaning's

instant     wild–
eyed as the cherry
tree blossoms

in that fanatic glass from our own
homes our own

rooms we are fetched out          we

*the greasers*
says yesterday's

slang in the path of tornado the words

piled on each other          lean
on each other dance

with the dancing

valve stems          machine glint
in the commonplace the last words

survivors, will be tame
will stand near our feet
what shall we say          they have lived their lives
they have gone feathery
and askew
in the wind from the beginning          carpenter
mechanic    o we
impoverished we hired
hands that turn the wheel          young
theologians of the scantlings          wracked
monotheists of the    weather-side   sometimes I imagine
they speak

◆     ◆

luxury,    all
said Bill, the fancy things          always

second hand but in extreme
minutes guilt

at the heart
of the unthinkable hunger          fear          enemy

world          briefly shame

of loneliness all that has touched
the man

touches him
again arms and dis–

arms him meaning
in the instant

tho we forget

the light

◆     ◆

precision of place the rock's place in the fog we suffer
          loneliness painlessly not without fear the common breath
                    here at extremity

obsolescent as the breathing
of tribespeople          fingers cold

early in the year cold and windy on the sea the wind
          still blows thru my head in the farmhouse

weather of the camera's click
lonely as the shutter closing
over the glass lens weathered mountains

of the hurrying sea the boat in these squalls sails
　　　　like a sparrow a wind blown
sparrow on the sea some kite string

taut in the wind green
and heavy the masses of the sea weeds move
and move in rock shelters share marvelous games

　　　　　◆　　　◆

inshore,　　　the rough grasses
rooted on the dry hills or to stand still

like the bell buoy　　telling

tragedy so wide
spread so

shabby a north sea salt
tragedy 'seeking a statement

of an experience of our own' the bones of my hands

bony　　　bony　　　lose me the wind cries　　find
yourself　　　I?

this?　　　　the road
and the travelling　　　　always

undiscovered
country forever

savage *the river*
*was a rain and flew*

*with the herons*      the sea
flies in the squall


        ◆    ◆


        backward
over the shoulder
now the wave
of the improbable
drains from the beaches the heart of the hollow
tree singing bird note bird rustle we live now
in dreams all
wished to tell him we are locked
in ourselves      That is not
what they dreamed
in any dream they dreamed the weird morning
of the bird waking mid continent

mid continent iron rails
in the fields and grotesque
metals in the farmer's heartlands a sympathy
across the fields
and down the aisles
of the crack trains
of 1918 the wave
of the improbable
drenches the galloping carpets in the sharp
edges in the highlights
of the varnished tables we ring
in the continual bell
the undoubtable bell found music    in itself
of itself speaks the word
actual heart breaking
tone row it is not ended
not ended the intervals

blurred ring
like walls
between floor
and ceiling the taste
of madness in the world        birds
of ice        Pave
the world o pave
the world carve

thereon . .

night—sky      bird's      world
to know    to know     in my life to know

what I have said to myself

the dark to escape in brilliant highways
of the night sky, finally
why had they not

killed me why did they fire that warning
wounding cannon only the one round I hold a
      superstition

because of this    lost to be lost    Wyatt's
lyric and Rezi's
running thru my mind
in the destroyed (and guilty) Theatre
of the War    I'd cried
and remembered
boyhood    degradation      other
degradations and this crime I will not recover
from that landscape it will be in my mind
it will fill my mind and this is horrible
death bed      pavement     the secret taste
of being lost

dead

clown in the birds'
world what names
(but my name)

and my love's name to speak

into the eyes
of the Tyger      blaze

of changes . . . 'named

the animals'      name

and name the vigorous dusty strong

animals gather
under the joists    the boards    older

than they    giving
them darkness the gifted

dark tho names    the names    the 'little'

adventurous
words    a mountain    the cliff

a wave are taxonomy I believe

in the world

because it is
impossible    the shack

on the coast

under the eaves
the rain barrel flooding

in the weather and no lights

across rough water illumined
as tho the narrow

end of the funnel what are the names
of the Tyger      to speak
to the eyes

of the Tiger     blaze
of the tiger     who moves in the forest leaving

no scent

but the pine needles' his eyes blink

quick
in        the shack
in the knife-cut
and the opaque

white

bread each side of the knife

INLET


Mary in the noisy seascape
Of the whitecaps

Of another people's summer
Talked of the theologians      so brave
In the wilderness she said      and off the town pier

Rounding that heavy coast of mountains
The night drifts
Over the rope's end

Glass world

Glass heaven

Brilliant beneath the boat's round bilges
In the surface of the water
*Shepherds are good people let them sing*

the little skirts life's breasts for what we can have
Is each other

Breath of the barnacles
Over England

over ocean

breakwaters      hencoops

# SEMITE

what art and anti-art to lead us by the sharpness

of its definitions connected
to all other things this is the bond

sung to all distances

my distances neither Roman

nor barbarian the sky the low sky

of poems precise
as the low sky

that women have sung from the windows
of cities sun's light

on the sills a poetry

of the narrow
end of the funnel proximity's salt gales in the narrow

end of the funnel the proofs

are the images the images
overwhelming earth

rises up

in its light nostalgia
of the mud guilts

of the foxhole what is a word a name at the
   limits

of devotion
to life the terrible knowledge

of deception

a lie told my loves tragically
pitifully had deceived

themselves had been betrayed

demeaned thrown away shamed
degraded

stripped naked Think

think also of the children
the guards laughing

the one pride the pride
of the warrior laughing so the hangman
comes to all dinners Aim

we tell each other the children cannot be
   alone whereupon murder

comes to our dinners poem born

of a planet the size

of a table top
garden        forest            an awning

fluttering four-lane

highway the instant

in the open the moving
edge and one
is I

# THE LITTLE PIN: FRAGMENT

*'The journey fortunately [said the traveller] is truly immense'*


of this
all things
speak if they speak the estranged

unfamiliar sphere thin as air
of rescue       huge

pin–point

cold little pin unresting
small pin of the wind and the rayne

in the fields the pines the spruces the sea and
       the intricate

veins in the stones and the rock
of the mountains wandering

stars in the dark their one
moral in the breeze

of wherever it is history
goes the courses and breaking

High seas of history . . . . Stagecraft
Statecraft the cast is absurd the seas
break on the beaches

of labor multitudinous
beach and the long cost

of dishonest
music

       Song?

astonishing

song?     the world
sometime be

world the wind
be wind o western
wind to speak

      of this

## THE LIGHTHOUSES

*(for L Z in time of the breaking of nations)*

*if you want to say no say*
*no if you want to say yes say yes* in loyalty

to all fathers or joy
of escape

from all my fathers I want to say

yes and say
yes the turning
lights

of oceans in which to say what one knows and to
limit oneself to this

knowledge is

loneliness turning and turning

lights

of safety for the coasts

are danger rock-pierced
fatalities far out  far out the structures

of cause

and consequence silver as
the minnows'

flash miraculous

as the seed sprouting
green at my feet among a distant

people therefore run away
into everything the gift

the treasure is

flight my
heritage *neither Roman*

*nor barbarian* now the walls are

falling the turn the cadence the verse

and the music essential

clarity plain glass ray
of darkness ray of light

# CONFESSION

'neither childhood
nor future

are growing less' guilts        guilts
pour in

to memory things leak I am an old ship
and leaky        oceans

in the bilges ordinary

oceans in the bilges I come to know it is so guilts
  guilts

failures in the creaking
timbers but to have touched

foundations keelson the cellars
as all this becomes strange

enough
I come to know it is home a groping

down a going
down middle-voice the burgeoning

desolate        magic        the dark
grain

of sand and eternity

## WHO SHALL DOUBT

consciousness

      in itself

of itself carrying

    'the principle
        of the actual' being

actual

itself ( (but maybe this is a love
poem

Mary) ) nevertheless

     neither

the power
of the self nor the racing
car nor the lilly

     is sweet but this

# TO THE POETS: TO MAKE MUCH OF LIFE

'come up now into
the world' no need to light

the lamps in daylight *that passion*
*that light within*

*and without*     (the old men were dancing

return
the return of the sun)     no need to light

lamps in daylight working year
after
year the poem

discovered

in the crystal
center of the rock image

and image the transparent

present tho we speak of the abyss
of the hungry we see their feet their tired

feet in the news and mountain and valley
and sea as in universal

storm
the fathers said we are old
we are shrivelled

come.

# TWO ROMANCE POEMS

*(for Jeremy Taylor)*

something wrong with my desk        the desk
the destroyer, desk is the enemy

bright light of shipwreck beautiful as the sea
and the islands I don't know how to say it
needing a word with no sound

but the pebbles shifting on the beach the sense
of the thing, everything, rises in the mind the
venture        adventure

say as much as I dare, as much as I can
sustain I don't know how to say it

I say all that I can        What one would tell
would be the scene        Again! !        power

of the scene I said the small paved area,
ordinary ground except that it is high above
the city, the people standing at a little distance
from each other, or in small groups

would be the poem

If one wrote it        No heroics, obviously, but
the sadness takes on another look

*as tho it mattered, in a way*
'smoke drifts from our hills'

◆        ◆

## RES PUBLICA: 'THE POETS LIE'

words, the words older
than I

clumsiest

of poets the rain's small

pellets        small

fountains that live
on the face

of the waters

dilations

of the heart they say
too much the heart the
heart of the republic skips

a beat where they touch it

# PRIMITIVE

## *(1978)*

## A POLITICAL POEM

for sometimes over the fields astride
of love?    begin with

nothing or

everything    the nerve

the thread
reverberates

in the unfinished

voyage loneliness

of becalmed ships and the violent men

and women of the cities'
doorsteps unexpected

this sad and hungry

wolf walks in my footprints fear fear
birds, stones, and the sun-lit

earth turning, that great

loneliness all

or nothing
confronts us
the image

the day

dawns on the doorsteps its sharpness
dazes and nearly blinds us

# DISASTERS

of wars o western
wind and storm

of politics I am sick with a poet's
vanity    legislators

of the unacknowledged

world *it is    dreary*
*to descend*

*and be a stranger* how
shall we descend

who have become strangers in this wind that

rises like a gift
in the disorder    the gales

of a poet's vanity if our story shall end
untold to whom and

to what are we ancestral *we wanted to know*

*if we were any good*

*out there*    the song
changes the wind has blown the sand about
and we are alone the sea dawns
in the sunrise verse with its rough

beach-light crystal extreme

sands dazzling under the near
and not less brutal feet journey
in light

and wind
and fire and water and air *the five*

*bright elements*
the marvel

of the obvious and the marvel
of the hidden is there

in fact a distinction dance

of the wasp wings dance as
of the mother-tongues can they

with all their meanings

      dance?   O

*O I see my love I see her go*

*over the ice alone* I see

myself   Sarah   Sarah   I see the tent
in the desert my life

narrows my life
is another I see
him in the desert I watch
him he is clumsy
and alone my young
brother he is my lost
sister her small

voice among the people the salt

and terrible hills whose armies

have marched and the caves
of the hidden
people.

## THE POEM

how shall I light
this room that measures years

and years not miracles nor were we
judged but a direction

of things in us burning burning for we are not
still nor is this place a wind
utterly outside ourselves and yet it is
unknown and all the sails full to the last

rag of the topgallant, royal
tops'l, the least rags
at the mast-heads

to save the commonplace save myself Tyger
Tyger still burning in me burning
in the night sky burning
in us the light

in the room it was all
part of the wars
of things brilliance
of things

in the appalling
seas language

lives and wakes us together
out of sleep the poem
opens its dazzling whispering hands

## TO MAKE MUCH

of the world of that passion

*that light within*
*and without*     no need

of lamps in daylight writing year
after
year the poem

discovered

in the crystal
center of the rock     image

and image     the transparent

present tho we speak of the abyss
of the hungry we see their feet their tired

feet in the news and mountain and valley
and sea as in universal

storm the fathers said we are old
we are shrivelled

come

·  ·  ·  ·

to the shining
of rails in the night
the shining way the way away

from home arrow in the air
hat-brim fluttered in the air as she ran
forward and it seemed so beautiful so beautiful
the sun-lit air it was no dream all's wild
out there as we unlikely
image of love found the way
away from home

## WAKING WHO KNOWS

the great open

doors of the tall

buildings and the grid

of the streets the seed

is a place the stone
is a place mind

will burn the world down alone
and transparent

will burn the world down tho the starlight is
part of ourselves

## IF IT ALL WENT UP IN SMOKE

*that smoke*
*would remain*

the forever
savage country poem's light borrowed

light of the landscape and one's footprints praise

from distance
in the close
crowd all

that is strange the sources

the wells the poem begins

neither in word
nor meaning but the small
selves haunting

us in the stones and is less

always than that help me I am
of that people the grass

blades touch

and touch in their small

distances the poem
begins

## THE TONGUES

of appearance
speak in the unchosen
journey immense
journey there is loss in denying
that force the moments the years
even of death lost
in denying
that force    the words
out of that whirlwind his
and not his strange
words surround him

## POPULIST

I dreamed myself of their people, I am of their people,
I thought they watched me that I watched them
that they

watched the sun and the clouds for the cities
are no longer mine     image     images

of existence     (or song

of myself?)     and the roads for the light
in the rear-view mirror is not
death but the light

of other lives tho if I stumble on a rock I speak
of rock if I am to say     anything          anything
if I am to tell of myself     splendor
of the roads     secrecy

of paths for a word like a glass

sphere encloses
the word opening
and opening

myself and I am sick

for a moment

with fear let the magic
infants speak we who have brought steel

and stone again
and again

into the cities in that word blind

word must speak
and speak the magic

infants' speech driving
northward the populist
north slowly in the sunrise the lapping

of shallow
waters tongues

of the inlets glisten
like fur in the low tides all that

childhood envied the sounds

of the ocean

over the flatlands poems piers foolhardy

structures and the lives the ingenious
lives the winds

squall from the grazing
ranches' wandering

fences young workmen's

loneliness on the structures has touched
and touched the heavy tools     tools
in our hands in the clamorous

country birth-
light savage

light of the landscape magic

page the magic
infants speak

# GOLD ON OAK LEAVES

*gold* said her golden

young poems for she sleeps and impossible
truths move

brave    thru    the gold    the living
veins but for the gold

light I am lost

in the gold

light on this salt and sleepless

sea I haunt an old

ship    the sun

glints thru ragged
caulking I would go out
past the axioms

of wandering

timbers garboards keelson the keel    full

depth

of the ship in that
light into all

that never
knew me alone

in the sea fellow
me feminine

winds as you pass

## THE NATURAL

world *the fog*
*coming up in the fields* we learned those
rural words later we thought it was ocean the flood
of the ocean the light
of the world help me I am

of that people the grass
blades touch

and touch the small

distances the poem
begins

## STRANGE ARE THE PRODUCTS

      of draftsmanship     zero
that perfect

circle

of distances terible
path

thru the airs small very
small alien

on the sidewalks thru the long
time of deaths

and anger

of the streets leading
only

to streets brutal pitifully

brutal the swaggering
streets you cannot

know all

my love of you o my dear
friend unafraid

in saturnalia    All
hallows Eve more

beautiful most
beautiful found

here saturnalia the poem
of the woman the man our dark

skull bones' joy in the small
huge dark the

glory of joy in the small
huge dark


      *—Polk St., Halloween, Oct. 31, 1976*

## NEIGHBORS

Thru our kitchen window I see the house
next door a frame house under the asphalt shingles
the wooden framing and I don't know what I am doing
here the neighbor the actual neighbor we are even
    friendly
in a way and I don't know what I am doing
here there is more
to wake to
than these old boards these many
boards and the voice of the poem a wandering
foreigner more strange
and brilliant
than the moon's       light the true
native opening
the nooks and the corners and the great
spaces clear
fields of her hands we
not poets only
waking all
are in her hands

          . . . . . . . . . .

    shall we
say more
than this I can
say more there it
is I can
say more we have hardly begun
to speak walk the round
earth for dark
truths and blazing
truths are the same they

move waver almost
stand in my
mind continually
in our
dreams like the shadows
of water
moving if
in time we see
the words fail this
we know this
we walk in and is all
we know we
will speak

to each
other we
will speak

## TILL OTHER VOICES WAKE US

the generations

and the solace

of flight memory

of adolescence with my father
in France we stared
at monuments as tho we treaded

water stony

waters of the monuments and so turned
then hurriedly

on our course
before we might grow tired
and so drown and writing

thru the night (a young man,
Brooklyn, 1929) I named the book

series empirical
series all force
in events the myriad

lights have entered
us it is a music more powerful

than music

till other voices wake
us or we drown

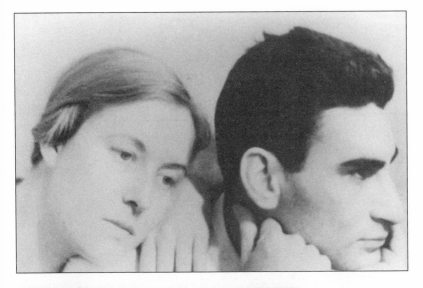

George and
Mary Oppen,
San Francisco,
1928
(photograph by
George Oppen, Sr.)

George and
Mary Oppen,
with Bucco
Zacheim, Jack,
and Zee Wag,
Paris, 1932

George Oppen on
board *Galley Bird*,
Long Island Sound,
1935

George and Linda
Oppen, Detroit, 1942

# UNCOLLECTED
# PUBLISHED POEMS

# POEMS 1932–33

**I**

This room,
             the circled wind
Straight air of dawn
                       low noon
The darkness. Not within
The mound of these
                  is anything
To fit the prying of your lips
Or feed their wide bright flowering.

And yet will movement so exactly fit
Your limbs——
         as snow
Fills the vague intricacies of the day, unlit:
So will your arms
                fall in the space
Assigned to gesture
      (In the momentless air
        The distant adventurous snow.)

**II**

When, having entered——
Your coat slips smoothly from your shoulders to the waiter:

How, in the face of this, shall we remember,
Should you stand suddenly upon your head

Your skirts would blossom downward

Like an anemone.


**III**

As I lift the glass to drink,
I smell the water: Suddenly,
The summer.

When my socks will be thick in my shoes

And the room's noise will go dim behind me
As I lean out a high window,

My hands on the stone.



**[BRAIN]**


Brain
All
Nuclei
Blinking
Kinetic
Electric sign
A
Pig
Dances
Painfully
Cannon
Rockets
A curve

Behind
This
Eye
No
Further brain;

The tendons
The slots
Pianola
Into slots
Sound
A room's
Back-
Ground

# POEMS 1960–81

## THE BIBLICAL TREE

Of life and knowledge.
Hand against the bole
She leans. Her eyes blur almost
With her love
Of bark above her hand.
His hand on solidness.
Head back, sees
Higher and then high

An air of branches, twigs, leaves;
High from the bole a city of the leaves

In future Spring!

              ——As gods!

But that the blood goes, yes,
In labor, in the long life job.


## MONUMENT


To exist; to be among things.
The art of nerve ends, masseur art
Of the blind skin.

Or the five
Senses gone
To the one sense, to well being

Lacks significance.
Or lacks life. The thing
By which the mind
Sees!——if it wake——

The wooden sills, the grimed past
Above the store fronts and the signs, the black

Telephone pole of the past sunned warm
As the tree's bulk, or the squirrel's

Eyes, whose substance, solid ounce, whose life
Bursts furious thru the leaves

     And down town,
The absurd stone trimming of the building tops
Rectangular in dawn, the shopper's
Thin morning monument.

## MEMORY AT 'THE MODERN'

We had seen bare land
And the people bare on it
And men camp
In the city. The lights,
The pavement, this important device
Of a race, I wrote then,
Twenty three years old,
Remains till morning. Nobody knows who died
On the roads of that time, of the fact of roads.
I am a man of the Thirties

'No other taste shall change this'

## A PREFACE

If he goes rowing in the park tho he may row so well that
      he seems to be ice-skating round the lake

He cannot go round that lake forever
An open voyage
Is another matter
It is his own affair
And he knows it

## VOYAGE

In the cabin. Here we have love.
On the closet hook
A jacket swings    swings like a pendulum


## FROM THE FRIENDLY LOCAL PRESS

There is a heavy plaster cast
On the young woman's leg. On the sidewalk she leans
On her husband's arm who walks
Slowly, leaning toward her,
Watching her steps. She laughs
And waves at a friend


## THE STUDENTS GATHER

The puddles
Shine with the sky's light

A Public Demonstration

Students gather in the square
Between two skies

Someone must speak

I too agree
We are able to live
Only because some things have been said

Not repeated

Said


## EPIGRAM


I have been insulted in St Peter's
Spat on in St Paul's
And hanged in the Place de la Concorde

There is one who admires my urbanity

One in the forest
Or one in the desert
Who envies my urbanity

It is true       and it is remarkable
Those old walls
Give shelter


## A MODERN INCIDENT


Culture
Of the draft-pool, an oblique poetry
Between speech and action

Between action and theatre
A pop culture
Of an elite
Engaged in revolt

Between art and environment,
Hedonist, a property of the young,
A popular song, a clean
Sweep


## THE THEOLOGICAL QUESTION


Thus desire
Becomes knowledge

Whether one loves
The world or loves
Shelter
From it

Is decisive, amnesiac children,
The dance of a death


## [ASTRAY OVER EARTH]


Astray over earth
Bright in darkness
Its light also a wandering foreigner.

## THE SONG

When the words *would*        *with*    *not*    *and*
Take on substantial Meaning
It is a poem

Which may be sung
May well be sung


## A POEM ABOUT THE GARDEN

      carpel
filament the brilliant
center pollen–gold

crimson stirs in a girl's
eyes as tho one had entered
a flower, and become a stranger


## A BARBARITY

We lead our real lives
in dreams one said meaning
because he was awake
we are locked in ourselves
That is not what he dreamed
in any dream
he dreamed the weird morning
of the bird waking

## ARTIST

he breaks the silence
and yet he hesitates, half unwilling

something comes to his mind
it is something about something

the sea

to ask
where is the sea he asks

where is the shore
he fears as the devil

himself his
cleverness

we move, we move, the mass of the people
moves is he trying to escape? to enter?


## THE LAW OF POETRY

rooted in the most unconscionable romance,
the words the thought the form and the music
for one's own sake: from this law is born the
law *and* the prophets. Or more simply.

## [BEAUTIFUL AS THE SEA]

beautiful as the sea
and the islands' clear light

of shipwreck the pebbles
shifting

on the beach that even sorrow

or most terrible

wound prove us part
of the world not fallen

from it the cadence the image
the poem is

conviction          forceful
as light


## [SYMPATHY]

                    sympathy          coincidence:    that the
meaning of the word *here* contains the meaning of
oneself
               And I am, as I've written somewhere, glad to be
here.

(or as I quoted Mary O saying when I read to her
Rilke's 'the animals and the insects /
stare at the open'   . . . therefore, said Mary, they
are welcome

## TO FIND A WAY

the turn the cadence the verse and the music,
clarity, plain glass and the slang word

speaks in the whirl wind the insulted

the challenged

blood of childhood now patriarchal
Jew most strange

to myself neither Roman

nor barbarian the words

and their strangeness saving

ray of strangeness ray
of exile.

ray of light


## GIFT: THE GIFTED

lighthouses    the turning the turning
lights

of safety the coasts

all danger    rock-pierced
fatalities    far out

miracle    miracle        the structure

'of cause and consequence becomes as it were

transparent'    silver

as the minnows'
flash

and still there is time there is time the common

unrolling I have time far-sighted

I think the miracle     miracle
of the seed         world's gift    gift

will sprout green at my feet as the miracle

of the myopic
will be distance    horizon

the fragile metallic

eye     penumbra
of the horizon

among the people
they have never spoken to therefore run away

into everything the gift

the treasure is

flight my
heritage

## EAGLES AND ALONE

once once only in the deluge

of minutes with the trees
the cities

a stone in the road waiting
stones, eagles, seagulls sliding

sideways down the wind I cannot find

a way to speak

of this the source
the image the space

of the poem our

space too great
or too small the translucent

woven

cloth of being
here the words

speak of too little

time remaining
fearful

of particles, eagles
and alone

## IMAGE

                        is a thinking a
choosing

(a politics) in the clear

air of all the worlds
precipices in the image of the poem
enters

itself the solitary
floors these hidden

floors in the bright ocean

light of the car's windows driving
northward the populist

north shoals in the low
tides glisten
like fur in the windless

morning tongues

of the inlets
stretch to the hills
feet in the sunrise the lapping

of shallow
waters the sounds

of the ocean
over the flatlands poems piers foolhardy

structures the lives the ingenious
lives the winds

squall from the grazing
herds at the skyline broad

winds of the white
ranches' wandering

fences young workmen's

loneliness on the structures has touched
and touched the heavy tools     tools
in our hands

## IN MEMORIAM CHARLES REZNIKOFF

who wrote
in the great world

small for this is a way

to enter
the light on the kitchen

tables wide-

spread as the mountains'
light this is

heroic this is
the poem

to write

in the great
world small

## [HE DE DARK]

he de dark
handsome

young man has

for her
de fair

maiden Uh

present,
de darling

## PROBITY

in the poem
or our hearts

will grow old
and break

## THE WHIRL WIND MUST

for the huge
events are the         symbols

of loneliness (a country

poem of the feminine) and children's

trinkets in the gravel
of the driveways the warm

blood flows
in her the hot

river in the drama
of things caught
in the face

of things village
things long

ago a wind destroyed

shelter     shelter more lonely
than suns

astray over earth music
in the dark music

in the bare light suddenly I saw
thru Carol's eyes the little road leading
to her house the trampled

countries of the driveways to face
the silence of the pebbles the whirl wind must

have scattered under the sun the scattered

words that we can muster where once
were the grand stairways

of sea captains                    language

in the roads speech

in the gravel the worn
tongues of the villages

## THE POEM

A poetry of the meaning of words
And a bond with the universe

I think there is no light in the world
but the world

And I think there is light

# SELECTED

# UNPUBLISHED POEMS

# POEMS FROM THE 1930s

## [THE PIGEONS FLY . . . ]

The pigeons fly from the dark bough
           unleaved to the window ledge;
There is no face.

## [PRECEDED BY MOUNTED POLICE]

Preceded by mounted police,
A band—
The corner-stone laid

The crowd on the civic pavement
See a new stone in turned ground.

## [STEAMER AT THE PIER]

Steamer at the pier,
Nose to the shore
A man walks the still decks

## [A LACED GAITER]

A laced gaiter
On the left fore-hook

Panoplied
To draw the hearse—

It evidently remains true that this horse,
born black-coated, toes in the right
fore-leg:
Detail of the corpse,
Hearse, bereavement.

# POEMS FROM THE 1950s TO THE 1970s

## FROM UP-STATE

The great church institutions
And a bill-board reading
Dine and Dance
Under the Stars
To Herman Morton's
Music.

The trade unionist in the car
With us—a friend—
Is furious against the churches
Which he says provide—
An opium—
As stated.

But if he hopes
For the general wealth
He talks of, if he does not want
Only dispute forever
He'll accept the bill-board's
Outlook

For all his hatred
Of the bourgeoisie and tho he
Can't dance.

And I cannot much longer bear
Sanity, I have been sane
A long time
or so it seems, seems sane
And seems a long time.


## MEMORY OF OARS


There are no nouns of verse, the earth itself
No longer home. A rocket into space——

And where the heart is,
Home. Water of the sea;
The leaping sea, or ground beneath the sea, beneath the
                    forest
Curving with the planet——Thrust
Thru the seas by the power of the oarsmen
They lowered the grapple over the bow again, shouting,
And caught a bottle out of the sea where it lapped up
                    and over in the bow wave
Glassy as the sea, for the message, addressed as always

To the shore or the ship, whole with the power of the
oarsmen.


## THE AMALGAMATED


Incredibly worn, the cafeteria of the fur workers and the
garment workers; they know each other, therefore they
know everything here, they have lived this life for a very
long time

It is an entirely terrible life

They are tired and possessed of endless energy; it must
be called courage

The hungry mosquito is courageous, you would let him eat
of you if only he would stay out of your ears

Or away from your head, you would let him eat, or you come
to think so

What does the mosquito think? He thinks he knows how to eat

Shall you love him for that? What is it that you want of
people, what is it that you want!


## THE COMFORTERS


Injured? Unenviable?
Ruined?

Failed! it is the last

Sound in the ears, the last
Buzz of the last fly.


## GENERATION OF DRIVERS


America, America,
Brand new America,
Old codgers' home,

'Fix anything', a village sign.
He tells them 'Treat 'er easy now.

Needs tires—'

Past it, thru it,
Down the highways, past the trailer camps
(They see them?  See the trailer camps?)
Half private down the eight lane roads,
The young
To find it—find their own.
But who the fathers?  How the sons?

And who loves who?

        An entity
Of two, and which they love?

## THE NEW PEOPLE

Crowding everywhere
Angrily perhaps
The world of stoops,
The new young people

With their new styles, the narrow trousers
Of the young men and the girls' bee hive
hair-do's this year they seem a horde

Who have invaded.
And they are, they are!
And each is someone: the tragic

Flaw. That they are not the real,
The virgin
Forest, wilderness,

The mineral,
From which they come.


## ACAPULCO

Walking the field
Before the battle in that play
The king's body's eyes looked down and saw
'This earth . . . this England'

Hear the tourists!
'Italy, the beaches are . . . '
(Athens, the martinis)

On these tourist beaches
The sun shines blinding on the sea that sparkles

## NEAR THE BEGINNING

Near the beginning was the horse.
Don't put the cart before the horse—
In all his ancientness and life,
Barn eyes gentle.

Strength and sweat and shyness,
Harness—

Whom children love that he's obedient and ancient
And strong, and greets them
From before all time and parents

And built the world of men and engines.

## NARRATIVE

How could those artists paint
The Virgin playing with her baby
In pure happiness?

The artist knows
How that story ended.
And the mother knows.

Still, they found models . . .

Tho in dreams
We see the craters of the moon.
We have our knowledge:

Structure of the gene, the evolution
Of the ground

Deeper in our lives, in our minds
Than any song, than any pictures.


## BELVEDERE


As I remember it, the harbor

Faced the orient;
The unused ferry slip
Stood in the harbor water

Like an outpost of the village

Growing old, the harbor waves
Lapped against   the pilings.


## REMBRANDT'S OLD WOMAN
## CUTTING HER NAILS


An old woman
As if one saw her now
For the first time, cutting her nails
In the slant light.

## TO THE MUSE

Nieves
Is a girl
From Scranton, Pennsylvania,
Came to San Francisco
To the poetry, the music, the cafes,
And art as Turkish Bath.

And had been told
A grandmother she's never seen in Mexico.
She goes

To visit that small village. Grandmother
A little woman ninety-two years old
Who greets her standing on a path
Before the house her father told her of

'A miracle', she says, 'One of my own.'

To this American young girl. So now you know, Nieves,
Now you know.

One likes to think of Nieves, twenty three years old
And small and slim in coffee houses and cafes
Who has her knowledge secret from those denizens
Of what a woman is.

## BRONX ZOO

The men have worked all week. If they have talked
    of desire

It was not of taking children to see the animals
Or to buy popcorn. They are embarrassed and ashamed:
They suspect they have fathered idiots
On the bodies of girls. They stare often into space
What are we waiting for?
What possibly can we be waiting for
Like penguins for some explorer to discover us?


[BILL BEFORE HIS DEATH]


Bill before his death
Bill very old
Still like a boy, but a boy
Whom an axe has hit
Again and again in the dark
In the last months, an arm
Stiff, a leg
Dragging, his speech
Impeded—'You cannot
Imagine', he said,
'What has
Been happening
To me—'


11/22/63


On 69th Street
They were weeping. A girl cried

Animals! Some
*An*imal!

For we are like him,
After all . . . And the young wife,
The very nice young wife,

Too nice
For the country . . . We are not the man

With the rifle,
Or feel we are not, we do

As seems right—nearly right—
And remain unarmed

Somehow,
We on 69th.

## A CULTURAL TRIUMPH

If 'Miss Moore's (birds) squeal, shuffle, lose their food
In the tree, in the mind, in the poem' as the critic
Reproduces them, is not
Something sound proven?——the bird
With its hard
Claws
Clinging to the rough
Tree, the small minds
In the trees,
The mind and the poem
Proven? Or is that not

What was in question? How terrible the mind
Is, open
To the world. The single mind
Flinches, panics, would, from its distance,
The too large body and its irremediable
Vision
Flood itself into the bird-life, but the poem observes
The bird from safety,
From the common culture.


## VISIT (1)


France is no longer
France, the farms
And the roads
Leading to their doors
That had so moved us
Traveling toward Paris
Half out of our childhood . . . It is pleasant
Leaning on the balustrade
Above the Seine,
A pleasant place. The courtyards
And the doors,
The curves in the road
Are quiet.
It is true I think I am Adam
As someone said
Where the animals
Have already been named
I want only
To go home.

## FLIGHT 162

       leaving from Idlewild, whose agents
Would, if need were, warn them,
Against such expedients as feathers
And winged horses.

Plain sons and daughters
Of plain fathers
Who have allowed the currents
Of events to form them
Sit side by side
In flight. My seat-mate
Reading the New Yorker
In mid-air as if to concentrate
Against my shoulder
The proof of their success, where others
With their wax and feathers failed.

## CHURCH INTERIOR

The stale room of religion,
Stale verification
Of the common ethic,

Of Keynesian economies,
The hushed core
embarrassed silence
The still place.

## MAUDIT

I can be stopped
Again anytime
By, shame.

The man sitting on his stoop, in a world of stoops, defeated;
What can anything I have written mean to him?
He does not know how he can live his life.

I can tell him nothing.
Unless perhaps he can think of his grandchildren
As if they were in some way himself,
And I know of no reason he should do so.


## MOUNT DESERT ISLAND

Two in the plastic cockleshell
Sailing by that coast of ponderous mountains

'Inflated landscape' someone had described it

And later at anchor in the busy
The minutely busy harbor

Mary talked of the Catholic theologians
'So brave in the wilderness'

Windy heaven of the poets
Where nostalgia and the new rise shining

## MOTHER AND CHILD

Theirs is the bond
Demonstrable.  Authority
In the blood
Still rebuilding
The baffling hierarchies
Of mother and child
To shield her
From time, from open
Time . . .

               something grows
Outward from forgotten roots,
Best forgotten, growing
Like the black branch
Out into space
From the incurable root, the most living
Green tip fed by a sap
The great black mass brings it, leafing
From the thin twig in new space.


## WHEELERS AND DEALERS: THE THEORY
##      OF GAMES

We might have foreseen it,
The triumph of calculation
The atom calculated
By its chances.
What can I know? What must I do?
What may I hope?
And what are my chances?

We ought to be able to survive it.
*Out of the unknown activities*
*Of unknown agents*
*Mathematical numbers emerge.* The last
Invisible world
Of the buyers, the sellers, the planners——

We ought to be able to survive it.


## THE PHONEMES


The poems have too much point
As tho I need invent
The thing in my mind always, available,
Juggler, why need I invent so much
Tho I think only of the coasts, figures of men and animals
On the silent coasts.


## LIGHT OF DAY


The sun
Slanting down
Toward evening

Lights the edge of a table
And two chairs
In the cafe

At the corner of McAllister

and MacDougall streets
And we are suddenly happy

Not for the warmth
But because the event
Is so large which has caused this.

'Lovely enchanting language, sugar-cane,
Hony of roses——' 'The stubborn rhetorical passion'
Stretched thinner than flame


## [THE OLD MAN]


The old man
In the mirror
Startles
Me
But the young man
In the photograph
Is stranger
Still.


## NATION


The whole city
Blazing light at evening——

One could picture him, the workman.
But the speedway's traffic;
Curved, enameled, glassed——

Even the factory is simple
Where they build these things
But the young woman in the car ahead
Is strange as an Etruscan vase——
And middle aged.
It grows confused.
The ten ton semi
Down the edge of pavement
Seems like some intrusion.

Grows confused.
The suburbs are a simple job. Foundations dug,
They could be dug with any shovel, worn out spade;
All that is simple. There is nothing in a house
That isn't simple; water glass, the roof, a house nailed tight
And in the window
Sun comes thru our things!

Burning
On the real horizon.
The million million windows of the city
And the grimed stills
Children, beds of the defeated,
The million weary wakings——

                                    These people poured
Into the enormous motion
As the day breaks on suburban shore


VISIT (2)


Sitting in your family apartment, Lewis,
Room of your apartment

Brooklyn Heights
The pictures and the breakfast nook
Were nice
And we two men
The men were talking
Glancing out the window.
                              In one glance
New York had disappeared
A wall of steel
An aircraft carrier dead slow
Advancing up the river
Like a building bigger than the rest
Point blank in front of our fourth story level
Planes I'll swear above us on the deck.
We felt like fools
We men, steel overshadowing
The works——the whole apartment


**THE EXTREME**


. . .   he talked of Hilton Hotels and quickie
        movies and his love affairs and I under-
        stood nothing at all
Perhaps I know nothing that I did not know when
        I was twenty


The pleasure of nostalgia


It is not one's position
Good or bad, but that I value so much the time
I have had
I treasure it to myself
I remind myself again and again

Of what I have witnessed and felt

The young do not yet possess so much time
It is not certain of any young man that he will.

Light grows, place becomes larger or deepens, the familiar
Becomes extreme

That the gate swings shut
That the wooden latch falls quietly
In this place, that the grass flows with the slope
Across the meadow
In this place to where the great trees stand

Or the familiar joy
Passing the hardware store
I remember the tools and the house
We once built
And the foundations, the stones and the thin worms
In the earth
The scratched metal edge of the shovel
So like another man's I knew even then I was not very young


## [PRESSES WERE BUSY ENOUGH]


Presses were busy enough
With no help from me
For twenty five years

Perhaps I was dealing nevertheless
With the essence of literature

To get down
Never the effort to go up

## VOLKSWAGEN

Of such deadly ancestry
The little car.
Small mirror and small wheels
Humming past the great cold farms
Of Normandy.

## THE DOG
### (An arrangement of a poem by Buddhaveda Bose)

Dog, don't look to me!
    The far seems far
    And the near near;
    The present silvers in the mirror.

Find yourself someone who starved
    And saw visions!
    At the least, never embarked
    On the great ships to England.

No? Do you think I will make
    Fantastic flute-like music
    For your sake, and stare in your eyes
    With memories of your birth?

Half of that I can do,
Big-eyed dog. But what you are
or were——the music
Is only the sound of music.

## ORPHEUS

The ship rounding
Scotland, islands
To the north

In polar mist
In the rather shallow sea——
Nothing more

But the sense
Of where we are

That seeks to find, to rescue
Love to the chill
Upper world, and to speak

A substantial language
Of dignity
And of respect.

## PARKWAY

If one had stumbled on these
Hard translucent flowers, the mind would move
Violently outward. But here is

World without end——
It was all true——a Sunday paradise
Of parkway, trees flowing into trees and the grass
Flows like water; the very asphalt crown

And summit of things
On which we move
thru the scrub of the past

In the family cars
Above old streets
And old boroughs          *ourselves*
*And things in the same moment*
Chairs and walls,
Floors, roofs, the joists and beams,
The woodwork, window-sills
Of bedroom fixed in a great work of brick.


**VALENTINE**


There are many of us,
There are very many,
Are they all us?


**US**


the finches at the feeder
in Spring yell

us us us us does their
language

contain
them

## SEMANTIC

There is that one word
Which one must
Define for oneself, the word
*Us*


## SAY

      I am

what
I am

whereupon curious

archangels

begin to watch


## A WIND MAKES UP

Grateful for a breeze
a breeze brings life
They are right, they are right
She falls off the wind
Somehow somewhere in the tubes
Of the television the sails fill, bubbles
Move along the hull
And we live, we speak darkly of storms

## WHAT WILL HAPPEN

There is a mobilization
We are all going to become handsomer
Richer more efficient more powerful
More loving than we are
I agree we know how

To do this is to enter a nightmare
From which we will be unable to awake

I have a different sense of myself

I am walking——no doubt like a lemming——
Northward    Some quirk            some tendency
Formed in childhood

Possibly the wrong direction
I want to know what will happen

I don't want to be cured
I don't want another and better wife
I don't want another and better daughter
Or other and better friends

Or to be cleverer than I am
Or even more admirable

Or outgoing    ingoing
Sidewinding I want to know

What I will be able to say
To myself       and I mean
To myself in my life

## THE RESOLVE

That there shall not be violence

Shelter

And there shall be no more death in the world

We would have resolved
That

If we could

The sacred individual
We say and do not mean it

Individuals do not last long enough

Free        Free

That we start from sleep
In horror

And cannot bear to speak of it


## THE SHORE

awaiting the
light to speak
of the present    which is
life to say to say to point
to requires a vividness    music    a
sound    Swim for what wood

what iron what plastic what ink
of the poem will come
ever here to this
shore to this sea


## SHE STEALS BIRDS


It is known.
She saw a baby chirping sparrow
In the grass and kneeled
To rescue him. The infant bird

Opened his beak wide
Dropped his wings and made
Little rushes at her finger
While his parents shouted from the bushes


## THE SPACE


In every bone
Of common ancestry the bird

Sees a tree
Where I do
And nests in it

Brood then
'in love and care'

Over this little space

STORY

A line of palm branch structures are along the beach
—    The tourists come

Hardwood posts are planted in the sand and roofed with palm
And passages marked out with stone and other structures,
        rooms and hallways,
White enameled tables to be walked around
Each with its bottle of Tabasco sauce, and all in sand

Out front are hammocks slung against the sea
For tourists. Children there, of course. They wash the dishes
In the ocean, lugging babies, bring the coconuts, and play.

All pretty children. Beautiful and brown.
But kids. The one is not.
A beauty or she will be, and she knows. Some miserable dream
Convinced her she's a foundling? Who knows how?

But made her sulky with the kids. She cries.
While we were there she cried three times
For nothing——insult, something, someone pushed

This beauty. Which she is.
Slim child and blazing black two eyes,
And this peculiar consciousness——from this small village
She will go into the city——with some man,
Of course——where she will blaze
With Indian beauty in some room

In anger. Who will know?
Know who she is?      The wind
That whips the palms and hisses

Ripples on the beach;
The children running on their round bare feet
In darkening light, and one is she.


## THE SQUIRREL'S STANCE


      explodes
From one posture to the next. The basic
Furry passion in an ounce. He has an air
Of playing house in air. His actual home
Must be a frenzy——squirrel frenzy

      Watched
By the two eyes from a tree is an experience
Of almost love.
His substance, solid ounce, his life
Burst furiously into leaves.


## [WITHOUT SELF-MUTILATION . . . ]


'Without self-mutilation there can be no withdrawing from
    our fellows'

Reading, I mis-read that. I thought: therefore we must accept
    mutilation

I will not answer. A man in war or a man tortured knows of
    another world.

They show him that his wife and his children have been killed.
    They were killed so easily.

There is not this world and that world.

The price of truth is ruinous. Rather redeem life, we mean
    rather to redeem life.


ANY WAY BUT BACK


I have a superstition of destiny. Those poets who have
lacked that superstition have died young

A superstition concerning families

Which is to say the future
Issuing from a dining room

And the old fashioned bulk
Of a family home.

Well, a madman.

Scenes
Still lucid

A child carried by the trains of nineteen–eighteen
From New York to California

Three thousand miles
Of rails

A *journey*, day's act
Redeemed 'outside all systems

Of redemption'
Its meaning formed in the veins

Of sympathy across the fields
To the gullies and the fences in the fields

And along the public aisles
In the train to the hushed doors

Of the diner
And the waiters

The men in the club car

Wild noise and grit
On the observation porch

And I did not know, when I was a child, whom to write to—
Handymen, servants, the primitive dead—

The book is my own. And, in a way, a deliberate surrender—
Those poems, the superstitious poems

To write the words down



**THE POWERS**


I would go home    o go home to the rough

stone become

the turn   the cadence    the verse and the music
          the essential

clarity,    plain glass,    strangest of all places

strange as all places strange as chance

strange as luck
and its guilts strange

strange and the slang word speaks
in the whirl-winds    Semite

to find a way

for myself now

old strange to happen
to a child strange

to become old the innocence

of the insulted in the challenged
blood of childhood now patriarchal

Jew most strange

to myself not Roman

nor barbarian had I foreseen
this the words

themselves
or their strangeness    strange

the saving ray
of strangeness    saving

ray of exile ray

of darkness ray of light


## ALL THIS STRANGENESS

it is a sea but is it music
binds

the spell

or thought    it is a sea

no place but the place
of desire the little boat runs up

against the long flank of the wave *shadow*

*brought into light* a place

like all others desire
desire at the heart of the living

world the poem

spells itself out *(why then
all this strangeness)* to say

all you know all
you are all
that has happened the world's

birth stirs like a breeze
in the streets and the lights
of the fast car

overtaking us
on the highway were the lights
of other lives dazzling silver

fire in the rear-view miror whitening

the grass if you look
deep

in the forest a girl's

poem said you may see
the poem
spells itself out


## A DREAM OF POLITICS

       in art

                in art

the image

need not declare itself the work of god yet I knew I
      would remember

children

running on the beach with their beating
hearts in the turn
of the seasons     small

pride small

terror in the soft dusk     centuries

behind these words here with the tongue and groove
wood of the back porch in the minor riot

of the grasses starlight
among us the night

becoming dawn

stitch upon stitch
sewn without thread bright

in the back yard     tongueless

as the neighborhood sleeping

sisters sleeping
brothers     dizzy

wordings o my elderly
siblings the children running

on the beach in the hissing
surf I don't know

don't know
what to say

## THE RESISTANCE

Partisan, she condemns
Only the victorious and gives herself
To the defeated and wanders in the fields

Of faith          as if there were something that could
Find her and approve her
Happiest wandering in the fields
her small feet touching the grass


## [A WOMAN, SAID DIANE . . . ]

A woman, said Diane, speaking wisely
Will let the boat drift
In the sun and the breeze
Let the boat drift
A man will grab an oar.
Perhaps he will
Any stick will do
To beat a father with


## THE POEM

          never
the chess game

the checker game
in which the pieces

have already been named

rather *inward*
and *outward*

under the sky.
This is the sky.


## THE DREAM


I dreamed one night that I was in Northern France in one
of the red-brick industrial towns the doors
and the windows locked. I knocked on a door and entered
and I said to the family    I *was here during the war, I was
in a house near here tho I cannot find it, it is near, you
can take me there they will know me.*   I stood
in that room and they would not guide me. I was lost and
they could not guide me

## MARY

her long quiet hands
sometimes it seems

almost strange it seems

sometimes the almost fifty years
has been a dream I hear sometimes those other

voices          voices

of my childhood
and fear I'll wake

Original manuscript page of an early draft of "Anniversary Poem," with
the title ("Heavy Handed As We Are") crossed out and a new one
("The Extremes") written in

# NOTES

# LIST OF ABBREVIATIONS

**A**       *Alpine*. Mont Horeb, WI: Perishable Press Ltd., 1969.

**CL**      *Contemporary Literature* 10:2 (Spring, 1969). "Objectivist Number."

**CP**      *Collected Poems*. New York: New Directions, 1975.

**CPF**     *Collected Poems*. London: Fulcrum Press, 1972.

**DS**      *Discrete Series*. New York: The Objectivist Press, 1934.

**GO**      George Oppen.

**GOMP**    *George Oppen: Man and Poet*. Ed. Burton Hatlen. Orono, ME: National Poetry Foundation, 1981.

**I**       *Ironwood* 26 (1985), "George Oppen: A Special Issue."

**JOD**     June Oppen Degnan, the poet's half sister.

**LO**      Linda Oppen, the poet's daughter.

**M**       *The Materials*. New York: New Directions, 1962.

**ML**      Mary Oppen. *Meaning a Life: An Autobiography*. Santa Barbara: Black Sparrow Press, 1978.

**MO**      Mary Oppen, GO's wife.

**NCP**     *New Collected Poems*. New York: New Directions, 2001.

**OBN**     *Of Being Numerous*. New York: New Directions, 1968.

**P**       *Primitive*. Santa Barbara: Black Sparrow Press, 1978.

**RBDP**    Rachel Blau DuPlessis, friend of George Oppen, poet, scholar, editor of GO's *Selected Letters*.

**S**       *Sulfur* 25 (Fall, 1989). "George Oppen: the Circumstances: A Selection of Uncollected Writing." Ed. Rachel Blau DuPlessis.

**SL**      *The Selected Letters of George Oppen*. Ed. Rachel Blau DuPlessis. Durham, NC: Duke University Press, 1990.

**SNE**     *Seascape Needle's Eye*. Fremont, MI: Sumac Press, 1972.

**TW**      *This in Which*. New York: New Directions, 1965.

**UCSD**    George Oppen papers, located at the Archive for New Poetry, Mandeville Department of Special Collections, University of California, San Diego Library (numbers following abbreviation refer to collection number, box number, file number).

# DISCRETE SERIES (1934)

*Discrete Series* was published by The Objectivist Press in 1934, with a preface by Ezra Pound. The poems were begun in 1929 when Oppen, then twenty-one, and MO were living in New York. Shortly after this period the couple, living on Oppen's inheritance, moved to southern France, settling in Le Beausset in the Var region, north of Nice. They returned from France in 1933 and with Zukofsky's help established The Objectivist Press, which published *Discrete Series*. After its publication (and in response to the Depression and growing political activism) Oppen stopped writing for twenty-five years.

The circumstance of *Discrete Series*'s composition is the subject of Oppen's last published poem:

> . . . writing
>
> thru the night (a young man,
> Brooklyn, 1929) I named the book
>
> series empirical
> series all force
> in events the myriad
>
> lights have entered
> us it is a music more powerful
>
> than music
> > (NCP, 286)

The nature of this "series empirical" is elaborated in Oppen's interview with L.S. Dembo:

> My book, of course, was called *Discrete Series*. That's a phrase in mathe-
> matics. A pure mathematical series would be one in which each term is
> derived from the preceding term by a rule. A discrete series is a series of
> terms each of which is empirically derived, each of which is empirically
> true. And this is the reason for the fragmentary character of those poems.
> I was attempting to construct a meaning by empirical statements, by
> imagist statements. (CL, 161)

In a letter to RBDP, Oppen felt the flyleaf "should have the inscription   14,  28,

32, 42  which is a discrete series: the names of the stations on the east side sub-way" (SL, 122). MO elaborates on this metaphor:

> We didn't yet know the subway system, and we got off at stations at ran-dom just to see what was above ground. Once we stuck our heads out into a cemetery, another time we were on clay fields with standing pools of water, and once we were among gigantic identical apartment build-ings in the Bronx, block after block. (ML, 89)

The first edition of DS printed each of its thirty-one poems on separate pages. This design feature was eliminated in the 1975 *Collected Poems*, as was the preface by Pound. Both are restored in this edition. The book was the subject of a review in *Poetry* in 1934 by William Carlos Williams, "The New Poetical Economy," which set forth many of the tenets for Objectivism:

> But this importance cannot be in what the poem says, since in that case the fact that it is a poem would be a redundancy. The importance lies in what the poem *is*. Its existence as a poem is of first importance, a tech-nical matter, as with all facts, compelling the recognition of a mechani-cal structure. A poem which does not arouse respect for the technical requirements of its own mechanics may have anything you please paint-ed all over it or on it in the way of meaning but it will for all that be as empty as a man made of wax or straw. (GOMP, 269)

Oppen published four poems under the title "Discrete Series" in the January 1932 edition of *Poetry*, of which only one, "Cat-Boat" (titled "The mast . . . ") appeared in the 1934 volume. Oppen also sent a typescript of the manuscript to Charles Reznikoff which included three poems that did not appear in the final version ("The pigeons fly . . . ," "Steamer at the pier . . . ," "A laced gaiter . . . "). A fourth poem, "Folie," was retitled "Drawing" in the final version. In the Reznikoff man-uscript, Oppen added a subtitle to the book, "The 1930s," which appears prior to the first poem and situates the series in the historical period of the Depression.

"THE KNOWLEDGE NOT OF SORROW, YOU WERE / SAYING . . . "
*Poetry* 37:5 (Feb. 1931), titled "1930's I"). In the Reznikoff typescript, this poem was preceded by the Roman numeral I. Above the Roman numeral was the sub-title, "The 1930's."

Maude Blessingbourne is a character in Henry James's "The Story in It," from which the quotation is taken. Oppen has added an "e" to her first name. In a letter to L.S. Dembo, Oppen says "I wanted James in the book [DS]—secretly, superstitiously, I carved his initials on that sapling book . . . " (SL, 241). The refer-ence to "boredom" announces a theme that will preoccupy the poet throughout his career. Although it is unlikely that he could have known it when he wrote this poem in the late 1920s, Oppen's concept of boredom anticipates Martin Heidegger's idea as stated in his acceptance speech for the chair of philosophy at Freiburg in 1929:

> Profound boredom, drifting here and there in the abysses of our exis-
> tence like a muffling fog, removes all things and men and oneself along
> with it into a remarkable indifference. This boredom reveals beings as a
> whole. (Martin Heidegger, "What Is Metaphysics." *Martin Heidegger:*
> *Basic Writings.* Ed. David Farrell Krell [New York: Harper & Row,
> 1977], 101.)

In his CL interview, GO paraphrases Heidegger: "The word 'boredom' is a little surprising there. It means, in effect, that the knowledge of the mood of boredom is the knowledge of what *is*, 'of the world, weather swept'" (CL, 169).

"WHITE, FROM THE . . . "
*Poetry* 37:5 (Feb. 1931), titled "1930's II." In *An Objectivists' Anthology*, this poem, along with the first and third poems of DS, is titled "1930s." The central image involves an ornamental device found over elevator doors during the period of the poem's composition. It is described in a 1963 letter to Charles Tomlinson:

> So familiar at the time that I don't think anyone was puzzled at the time.
> Printed c 1930 in Poetry. The office building evoked by its lighting
> effects in those dim days. And its limited alternatives, the limited alter-
> natives of a culture. (SL, 90)

GO continues by providing a sketch showing a T-shaped design, with two globes below each of the cross bars, one indicating "up" and the other "down."

"THUS / HIDES THE . . . "
In an "addenda" to a typescript draft of "Orpheus" ("Selected Unpublished Poems," NCP, 334) Oppen provides a gloss on the reference to the Frigidaire:

> To masturbate is to convince oneself that a cushion is a pretty girl. To
> masturbate is to call a pretty girl—anything else but that. Or to call
> the desire to be loved back—anything more or less than that. To inflate
> or to treat with contempt—is onanism.
> So is fancy language.
> And 'the prudery
> Of Frigidaire'

(UCSD, 16, 1, 4)

"THE MAST / INAUDIBLY SOARS . . . "
*Poetry* 39:4 (Jan. 1932), titled "Cat-Boat," a reference to the small boat taken by Mary and George Oppen from Detroit through the Great Lakes, Erie Canal, and down the Hudson River to New York in 1928.

"CLOSED CAR—CLOSED IN GLASS——"
In his CL interview, GO speaks of the image of the closed car: "There is a feeling of something false in overprotection and over-luxury—my idea of categories of realness" (CL, 168).

"WHO COMES IS OCCUPIED . . . "
In his interview with L.S. Dembo in GOMP, Oppen comments on the last four lines: "That's specifically something I've said since, I think, of the vision of the raw land under that asphalt. There's the asphalt but under it is really what was, or even is, just a prairie, just the raw land" (GOMP, 200).

"PARTY ON SHIPBOARD"
One of two titled poems in DS, "Party on Shipboard," occupies a particularly important place in Oppen's thinking about the series, as evidenced from a 1934 letter to Pound: "The book'll be named *Discrete Series*. Tricky, but I want a name out of statistics for 'Party Aboard' and some others particularly, and the term describes my hon. intentions pretty accurately" (SL, 4). In a letter to JOD, Oppen says, "I was really kind of moved to see I'd written a statement, and a very clear one, of what I was going in search of when I quit writing—the Party on Ship-Board" (SL, 20).

"TUG AGAINST THE RIVER—"
Omittted from CPF.

"SHE LIES, HIP HIGH, . . . "
Omittted from CPF.

"CIVIL WAR PHOTO:"
Apparently Oppen thought of eliminating this poem. Writing to Pound in 1934, GO says, "Poem with this [copy of *Discrete Series*]—sorry I didn't get it in to replace Civil war photo." The poem he included is "Preceded by mounted police" ("Selected Unpublished Poems," NCP, 313).

"FRAGONARD,/ YOUR SPIRAL WOMEN . . . "
Jean Honoré Fragonard (1732–1806), French rococo painter who often painted portraits of women in bucolic settings.

In an interview with Burt Hatlen and Tom Mandel, GO says that the opening line is derived from Ben Jonson (GOMP, 43).

Drawing
Under the title "Folie," this poem concludes the Reznikoff typescript version.


# THE MATERIALS (1962)


*The Materials* was the first book that GO published after the twenty-five year silence following the writing of *Discrete Series*. It was published in 1962 by New Directions in its San Francisco Review series, edited by Oppen's sister, June Oppen Degnan. The poems for the new volume were begun in 1958 while the poet was living in Mexico, where he and his wife had moved in 1950 to escape the anti-Communist witchunts. During this period, GO worked with a partner in a furniture manufacturing business and later, with MO, attended art school on the "G.I. Bill." In 1958 GO had a significant dream, which he subsequently referred to as the "Rust in Copper dream," and which aided his return to writing (see Introduction, xxi). The return to writing coincided with other factors, domestic and historical, that brought the couple back to the United States. Their daughter, Linda, entered Sarah Lawrence College in 1958, and the climate of U.S. politics had shifted away from the extreme paranoia of the McCarthy era, enabling the Oppens to obtain passports and move more freely across the U.S.–Mexico border.

Although they visited their daughter in 1958, they returned to Mexico several times, spending time in Acapulco, where a number of poems in this volume were written The final move to Columbia Heights, in Brooklyn, occurred in May 1960. Some sense of his impatience at getting back to his writing can be gleaned from a letter to JOD 1961 in which GO discussed his proposed volume: "The important thing for me is to get this group out, away, finished, off my mind. I'm having trouble getting further—and these *should* have been written in 1940" (SL, 379, n.1).

The title, *The Materials*, would seem to refer to Oppen's lifelong concern with the primary elements of experience, those "little nouns that he [liked] the most" (CL, 162). As the first book published after twenty-five years of silence, its title also refers to values of work, family, and community that sustained him through the ideologically charged 1930s and 1940s as well as the period of exile in 1950s. In this book, concerns over global geopolitics (for example, the Cold

War missile crisis in "Time of the Missile" or the specter of nuclear holocaust in "The Crowded Countries of the Bomb") expand Oppen's materialist critique of capitalist exploitation to include a new kind of political dominance, one involving giant superpowers and new forms of media and technology. At the same time, the title refers to the carpentry and furniture-building work that GO had been doing in Mexico, as well as the concern which he shared with other Objectivists with poetry *as* material, the "lyric valuables" that constitute a world.

Epigraphs: "We awake in the same moment to ourselves and to things": a misquotation from Jacques Maritain, *Creative Intuitition in Art and Poetry*: "Now if it is true that creative subjectivity awakens to itself only by simultaneously awakening to Things...." In his own copy of this book, Oppen has written: "Things: that things resound in him, and that in him, at a single wakening, they and he come forth out of sleep" (see Peter Nicholls, *George Oppen and the Fate of Modernism*. New York: Oxford University Press, 2007). "They fed their hearts on fantasies / And their hearts have become savage": a misquotation of Yeats's poem, "The Stare's Nest By My Window," the sixth poem in his sequence, "Meditations in Time of Civil War." The poem's final stanza reads as follows:

> We had fed the heart on fantasies,
> The heart's grown brutal from the fare;
> More substance in our enmities
> Than in our love; O honey-bees,
> Come build in the empty house of the stare.

> *The Poems of W.B. Yeats.* Ed. Richard J. Finneran (New York: Macmillan, 1983), 205.

ECLOGUE

GO describes this as "my version of a bucolic poem, a rural scene, looking out the window [where] humans [talk] of deals and triumphs as a kind of artillery bombardment against that indestructible natural world" (GOMP, 205). The poem is based on Virgil's Fourth Eclogue, which is addressed to a newborn boy and which was understood by the medieval world to be a prophecy of Christ's coming:

> incipe, parve puer, risu cognoscere matrem;
> matri longa decem tulerunt fastidia menses.
> incipe, parve puer; cui non risere parentes,
> nec deus hunc mensa, dea nec dignata cubili est.

> Begin, baby boy, to know thy mother with a smile—to thy mother ten months have brought the weariness of travail. Begin, baby boy! Him on whom his parents have not smiled, no god honours with his table, no

goddess with her bed!

Virgil, *Eclogues, Georgics, Aeneid I-VI*. Trans. H. Rushton Fairclough (Cambridge: Cambridge University Press, 1967), 33.

See also "From Virgil," which features variants on lines in this poem: "O small boy,/ To be born" (NCP, 105).

IMAGE OF THE ENGINE
See interview in GOMP, 205-7.
"*Also he has set the world / In their hearts*": from Ecclesiastes 3:11. The King James version reads as follows: "He hath made every thing beautiful in his time: Also he hath set the world in their heart, so that no man can find out the work that God maketh from the beginning to the end."

POPULATION
Probably written in Acapulco, Mexico.

RESORT
*Shake the Kaleidoscope: A New Anthology of Modern Poetry*. Ed. Milton Klonsky (New York. Pocket Books, 1973). "a volcano snow-capped in the air . . . ": reference to the Oppens' home in Mexico where they lived in the 1950s, although the address on an early draft (entitled "The Retirement") is 169 Columbia Heights, Brooklyn, New York. (UCSD 16, 20, 10).

TRAVELOGUE
*Poetry* 99:6 (Mar. 1962). Called "The Undiscovered Country" in CPF.

RETURN
Early draft titled "Acapulco" begins:
>Walking the field
>Before the battle in that play
>The king's body's eyes looked down and saw
>'This earth . . . this England'
>Hear the tourists!
>'Italy, the beaches are . . .
>(Athens, the martinis)
>
>On these tourist beaches
>The sun shines blinding on the sea that sparkles
>>(UCSD 16, 20, 46)
A second variant, titled "Pro Vita," begins:

Turning and turning in the broken streets
One hundred million desperate.
What mattered were the hungry.
So they felt
Surely verse can be an insolence: *What is the war*
*But an extension of the dance?*

(UCSD, 16, 20, 46)

"*This Earth . . . This England . . .* ": from Shakespeare, *Richard II*, II:1. John
of Gaunt, Duke of Lancaster, is dying. He delivers a patriotic speech to his broth-
er, Duke of York, on the tragedy of Britain weakened by actions of his nephew,
King Richard. Petra: Petra Roja. Friend of the Oppens and social activist in New
York during the 1930s (see ML, 153-54). "Coughlin": During the 1930s, Father
Charles Edward Coughlin broadcast *The Golden Hour of the Little Flower* on CBS
radio, a forum attacking Communism, Wall Street bankers, and Jews. "Pelley and
the Silver Shirts." William Dudley Pelley, a Hollywood writer and anti-Semite,
organized a U.S. Fascist movement, the Silver Shirts, during the late 1930s.
"Ceremony of Innocence": from W. B. Yeats, "The Second Coming": "The blood-
dimmed tide is loosed, and everywhere / The ceremony of innocence is
drowned"(*The Poems of W.B. Yeats,* ed. Richard Finneran [New York: Macmillan,
1983], 187).

"FROM DISASTER"

*Jewish-American Literature: An Anthology.* Ed. Abraham Chapman (New York:
Mentor/New American Library, 1974). "From disaster / Shipwreck": the first of
several references to Daniel Defoe's *Robinson Crusoe*. See also "Of Being
Numerous" 7: "Obsessed, bewildered // By the shipwreck / of the singular . . . "
(NCP, 166).

"SARA IN HER FATHER'S ARMS"

*The New Naked Poetry: Recent American Poetry in Open Forms.* Eds. Stephen Berg
and Robert Mezey. (Indianapolis: Bobbs-Merrill, 1976). Sara: daughter of Max
Pepper (1930–), friend of the Oppens, director of Mental Health Planning in
Connecticut and later professor in Community Medicine, St. Louis School of
Medicine.

BLOOD FROM THE STONE

Part IV in *Inside Outer Space: New Poems of the Space Age*. Ed. Robert Vas Dias
(Garden City, New York: Doubleday /Anchor, 1970). In his interview with L.S.
Dembo GO says that "Blood from a Stone" was the first poem that he wrote while
in Mexico upon returning to poetry (CL, 176). In an earlier draft, the poem is titled
"To Date," and is misdated "January 1949" (UCSD 16, 1,1). On the Oppens' work

in relief organizations during the 1930s, see ML, 152-55.

BIRTHPLACE: NEW ROCHELLE
*Poetry* 95:4 (Jan. 1960). *Shake the Kaleidoscope: A New Anthology of Modern Poetry.* Ed. Milton Klonsky (New York: Pocket Books, 1973). Oppen was born in New Rochelle, New York, April 24, 1908.

MYSELF I SING
*Poetry* 95:4 (Jan. 1960). The opening lines refer, perhaps ironically, to Walt Whitman's "One's-Self I Sing," which inaugurates all editions of *Leaves of Grass* after 1871. "'Incapable of contact / Save in incidents'": see "Party on Shipboard" in DS (NCP,15).

STRANGER'S CHILD
*Chicago* (Oct. 1973). "Chaucer's bird. . . . ": a possible reference to Chaucer's *The Parlement of Foules* which describes the sparrow:

> The sparwe, Venus sone; the nyghtyngale,
> That clepeth forth the grene leves newe;
> The swalwe, mortherere of the foules smale
> That maken hony of floures freshe of hewe; (351-54)

> *The Works of Geoffrey Chaucer.* Ed. F. N. Robinson (Boston: Houghton Miffflin Co., 1957), 314.

Chaucer's *The Parlement of Foules* begins, "The lyf so short, the craft so long to lerne," a phrase often quoted by Pound and Zukofsky.

OZYMANDIAS
*The Crowell College Reader.* Ed. Sheridan Baker and David B. Hamilton (New York: Crowell, 1974). *Our Own Thing: Contemporary Thought in Poetry.* Ed. Gretchen B. Crafts (Englewood Cliffs, NJ: Prentice-Hall, 1973). Omitted from CPF. Ozymandias: Tyrant of Shelley's poem by that name.

DEBT
*San Francisco Review* 7 (Dec. 1960). In a letter to JOD of 1963 or '64, Oppen considered eliminating this poem, were he to publish a "collected works" (CL, 98). Originally titled "The Manufactured Part" (UCSD 16, 20, 19). The *San Francisco Review* version reads as follows:

> So let us speak, and with some pride, of other men.
> Not passengers; the crew.

Or the machine shop. For the planet
Isn't habitable but by labor—

We are alone and live by labor—
Benches, and the men,
The noise, the shock
Of the press where for an instant on the steel bed,
The manufactured part!

New.
Newly made. Imperfect, for they made it; not as perfect
As the die they made which was imperfect. Checked
By some mechanic. What percent
Of human history, so little said of it.

PRODUCT
*Maine Lines: 101 Contemporary Poems About Maine.* Ed. Richard Aldridge
(Philadelphia: Lippincott, 1970).

WORKMAN
GO worked as a house-builder and carpenter while living in Mexico during the
late 1950s.

THE UNDERTAKING IN NEW JERSEY
*The Massachusetts Review* 3:2 (Winter, 1962).

TOURIST EYE
Written or typed in Acapulco, Mexico (address on draft reads "Dragos 56,
Acapulco, Gro."). Section 3 originally titled "The Wilshire Arms" (UCSD, 16, 20,
46). Lever Brothers: glass-front skyscraper in Manhattan, designed by Skidmore,
Owings and Merrill, the epitome of International Style modernism. Red Hook: a
working-class neighborhood in Brooklyn near the Oppens' home. "The necessary
city": In a letter to Denise Levertov, GO says, "Like to urge you again to come look
out our attic window sometime. That is, we could look out amicably in our sev-
eral ways at 'the necessary city'" (SL, 80).

VULCAN
Vulcan: son of Jupiter and Roman god of fire and metalworking, patron of hand-
icrafts and forging. Crippled as a result of being thrown out of Mt. Olympus by
his father for having taken the part of his mother, Juno. Identified with the Greek
Hephaestus.

FROM A PHOTOGRAPH
Family photograph of GO and his daughter in album dated January 1943 (UCSD FB 094). See illustration, NCP, 288.

THE TUGS OF HULL
Omitted from CPF. Hull: a seaport in northeastern England. "The man with the domestic pitcher pouring the Ganges / Back": refers to people who live by the river Ganges in India, whose morning devotional worship (*puja*) consists in making offerings of colored powder or flowers to the river. This ritual always involves filling a pitcher with river water and then pouring it back.

TIME OF THE MISSILE
GO discusses this poem and the escalating Cold War in a letter to Julian Zimet in 1959 (SL, 27-30).

THE MEN OF SHEEPSHEAD
Sheepshead: a town at the south end of Brooklyn, east of Coney Island, on Sheepshead Bay.

ANTIQUE
*San Francisco Review* 7 (Dec. 1960).

COASTAL STRIP
Written in Acapulco, Mexico.

O WESTERN WIND
Title refers to an anonymous 15th-century lyric quoted in several of GO's poems.

THE HILLS
Omitted from CPF. Written in Acapulco, Mexico.

THE SOURCE
*Poetry* 95:4 (Jan. 1960). An early draft titled "A woman":

> Tho the dawn rise
> Each day beyond the window, her voice awakes
> The door, the walls, the very floors which have become
> Herself and which she has become
> Against the future and the terrible broad day,
> The broad field and the old man
> Crying *Absolon* . . . [sic]
>
> (UCSD 16, 20, 31)

CHARTRES
Poem discussed in letter to John Crawford, 1973 (SL, 253-54). The Oppens visit-
ed Chartres Cathedral in the early 1930s and read Henry Adams's account in
*Mont St. Michel and Chartres*. See ML, 134.

DAEDALUS: THE DIRGE
Original title, "Bobby."

PART OF THE FOREST
*Poetry* 95:4 (Jan. 1960).

SURVIVAL: INFANTRY
*Our Own Thing: Contemporary Thought in Poetry*. Ed. Gretchen B. Crafts
(Englewood Cliffs, NJ: Prentice-Hall, 1973). Oppen served in the infantry in
World War II in France, where he survived a violent shelling.

CALIFORNIA
Omitted from CPF. Palos Verdes: a penninsula that extends into the Pacific Ocean,
south of Los Angeles.

SUNNYSIDE CHILD
Omitted from CPF. Sunnyside is a neighborhood in Queens, New York.

PEDESTRIAN
Retitled several times: "Young Pedestrian," "Grandchild," and "Young Winter."

TO MEMORY
*San Francisco Review* 10 (Dec. 1961). Omitted from CPF. Buddhadeva Bose:
Bengali poet and friend of the Oppens. GO wrote a series of variations on Bose's
poems that were translated in the magazine *Kadiva*. See also "Still Life" (NCP, 88)
and "The Dog" (NCP, 333) in "Selected Unpublished Poems."

STILL LIFE
*Chicago* (Oct. 1973). See note to "To Memory" above.

LEVIATHAN
In an early draft, the poem is preceded by an epigraph by "Steven S[chneider]," a
writer and friend of the Oppens whom they met in Mexico: "Happiness is the
pursuit of it." Hence the opening line's variation (UCSD 16, 20, 42). Leviathan:
biblical sea-serpent. Thomas Hobbes used Leviathan as the title of his political
treatise on "the Matter, Form and Power of a Commonwealth Ecclesiastical and
Civil" (1651).

# THIS IN WHICH (1965)

Writing to JOD in 1963 or '64, GO remarked that the poems in his new manuscript (to be called *This in Which*) "contribute only to the process which is stripping people of their defenses" (SL, 98–99). This austere ethos is embodied in many of the poems and certainly in the second of the book's epigraphs, a quotation from Martin Heidegger, who defines the philosophical necessity of pursuing "the arduous path of appearance." *This in Which* was published, like its predecessor, *The Materials*, by New Directions in its *San Francisco Review* series. The poet's sister, June Oppen Degnan, is acknowledged in the dedication, "For June / Who first welcomed / me home," which alludes to her role in publishing GO's previous book when he returned "home" to poetry after his twenty-five-year silence. Originally the book was to have an epigraph from St. Thomas Aquinas's *Veritas sequitur esse rerum* ("Truth follows from the being of things"), but this was ultimately dropped, although it appears piecemeal in several poems in the volume (SL, 98).

Epigraphs. The first epigraph comes from Robert A. Heinlein's novel *The Unpleasant Profession of Jonathan Hoag*. The second comes from Martin Heidegger's *An Introduction to Metaphysics:*

> Superior knowledge—and all knowledge is superiority—is given only to the man who has known the buoyant storm on the path of being, who has known the dread of the second path to the abyss of nothing, but who has taken upon himself the third way, the arduous path of appearance. (Martin Heidegger, *An Introduction to Metaphysics*. Trans. Ralph Manheim. [New York: Doubleday/Anchor, 1961], 96)

In a letter to RBDP, GO summarized the meaning of the title:

> This in Which means what it means in the Psalm [a poem in the book]. But contains some private amusements in that it means also the achievement of form; that the materials in achieving solidity, form, appear in the light of the miraculous. Or so I mean them to. —And I don't mean to write the same book again. (SL, 122)

As Norman Finkelstein observes, *This in Which* is Oppen's "most explicitly politicized" book, one which "examines the limits of bourgeois ideology in contrast to his own sense of ethics, based upon long years of political praxis" (GOMP, 360). The book includes poems concerning the Cold War, the assassination of John F.

Kennedy ("Armies of the Plain"), the excesses of wealth ("Guest Room," "A Language of New York," 1), and the poverty of the 1930s ("Street"), as well as memories of military action in World War II ("A Language of New York," 3).

TECHNOLOGIES

A response to a poem by Denise Levertov, "Who Is at My Window" (*O Taste and See* [New York: New Directions, 1964], 50-51), about which GO has written,

> After a bitter argument with me, Denise Levertov wrote a poem in which a hawk howls on the window sill. 'Nothing matters, *timor mortis conturbat me*' and so on. I think Denise was pretty mad at me. I was pretty mad at her when I wrote this poem, too, and said so I'm a hawk, and so forth. But as for the feminine technologies . . . the feminine technologies I take to be a kind of medical pragmatism . . . There are times one is infinitely grateful for the feminine contribution, and times one just has to fight about it, and this poem was more or less fighting. (GOMP, 209)

ARMIES OF THE PLAIN

The title condenses materials from two lines of Matthew Arnold's "Dover Beach": "Where ignorant armies clash by night," and "we are here as on a darkling plain." A letter to Charles Tomlinson describes the poem as follows: "Armies of the Plain—To make a clean breast of this matter, one means to refer to Arnold— –'Where ignorant armies clash by night.'" (SL, 387, n. 17) The poem is a response to the assassination of John F. Kennedy, on November 22, 1963. Quotations are drawn from the Warren Report on the assassination, particularly remarks by Jack Ruby about Oswald's being "A zero, a nothing'" and about Ruby's need to respond to the assassination as a "man of the Jewish faith." See letter to Linda Oppen (Mourelatos) and Alex Mourelatos, September 30, 1964, which discusses the report in detail, analogizing the events in Dallas to Joyce's *Ulysses* (SL, 106-8).

PHILAI TE KOU PHILAI

*Poetry* 102:4 (July 1963). Title taken from Euripides' *Electra*: "Here, one loved and not loved, / we cover with these veils" (ll. 1230-31). This translation is included in a postcard to GO from Alex Mourelatos, January 1963 (UCSD 16, 1, 21). Inspiration for the title came from GO's viewing of the film of *Electra* starring Irene Papas in New York, December 1962 (SL, 381, n. 23). "There is a portrait by Eakins / Of the Intellectual": Refers to Thomas Eakins's *The Thinker*, a portrait of Louis N. Kenton, 1900, currently at the Metropolitan Museum of Art. "Charles" is Charles Humboldt (1910–64), a friend of the Oppens in Mexico, later the editor of *The New Masses* and *Mainstream*.

PSALM

*Agenda* (England) 4:3-4 (1966). *Chicago* (Oct. 1973). *Poetry* 102:4 (July 1963). *The New Naked Poetry: Recent American Poetry in Open Forms.* Eds. Stephen Berg and Robert Mezey (Indianapolis: Bobbs-Merrill, 1976). Epigraph: "*Veritas sequitur . . .*" See headnote to *This in Which.* The phrase *Veritas sequitur esse rerum* (*Truth follows upon the existence of things*) is discussed in Jacques Maritain's *Existence and the Existant.* In his chapter on 'Being' Maritain explains that the phrase deals with "those trans-objective subjects with which thought stands face to face. Truth is the adequation of the immanence in act of our thought with that which exists outside our thought. True knowledge consists in a spiritual super-existence by which, in a supreme vital act, I become the other as such, and which corresponds to the existence exercised or possessed by that other itself in the particular field of intelligibility which is its peculiar possession." L.S. Dembo asked Oppen, "What exactly is the faith? [as it appears in 'Psalm']," to which Oppen responded:

Well, that the nouns do refer to something; that it's there, that it's true, the whole implication of these nouns; that appearances represent reality, whether or not they misrepresent it: that this in which the thing takes place, this thing is here, and that these things do take place. On the other hand, one is left with the deer, staring out of the thing, at the thing, not knowing what will come next. (CL, 163)

THE *CITY OF KEANSBURG*
Omitted from CPF. Keansburg, located on the Lower New York Bay, south of Brooklyn. The fact that the phrase occurs in italics suggests that this is also the name of a ship, possibly "the excursion steamer / Which carried us / In its old cabins . . . ," referred to in the poem.

FIVE POEMS ABOUT POETRY
Poem 4, "Parousia," called "The Last Day" in CPF. "The little hole in the eye . . .": from William Carlos Williams, "Shadows" II, from *Journey to Love* (1955):

> Save for the little
> central hole
> of the eye itself
> into which
> we dare not stare too hard
> or we are lost.

*The Collected Poems of William Carlos Williams* Vol. II: 1939–1962. Ed. Christopher MacGowan (New York: New Directions, 1988), 310.

Parousia: in the New Testament, refers to the Second Coming of Christ. According to John Taggart, GO also drew on Alex Mourelatos' interpretation of the Greek word as "presence" (John Taggart, "Walk Out: Rereading George Oppen" *Chicago Review* 44:2 [1998]: 39). Poem 5: "'life is a search / For advantage.'" From Aleksandr Sergeyevich Yesenin-Volpin, A Leaf of Spring. Yesenin-Volpin was a Russian poet and logician, the son of the lyric poet, Sergey Yesenin, His writings led to his arrest in 1949, and he spent several years in prison. In "A Free Philosophical Treatise,"Yesenin-Volpin says, "Thought consists in a search for truth; life, in a search for advantage. These two ideals represent opposite poles to anyone who must choose between them." " 'At whose behest // Does the mind think?' ": from the Kena Upanishad section 1, line 1."*Parve puer . . .*": from Virgil Eclogue IV. See note to "Eclogue" (NCP, 39)."the sky / was over Gethsemane, / Surely it was this sky." In an earlier draft, a variant of these lines was part of a separate poem, "From the Work of Charles Reznikoff":

> 'The telephone numbers we remember
> And which it would be useless . .
> To call'

> This is the sky
> Which was over Gethsemane—
> Surely it was this sky

>            ' . . . the girder
>     still itself . . . '
>                                 (UCSD, 16, 1, 9)

THE FORMS OF LOVE
*Chicago* (Oct. 1973). *Poetry* 102:4 (May 1964). *The New Naked Poetry: Recent American Poetry in Open Forms.* Eds. Stephen Berg and Robert Mezey (Indianapolis: Bobbs-Merrill, 1976). *Loves, Etc.* (Garden City, NY: Doubleday/Anchor, 1973). Asked about the meaning of this poem, Oppen replied to L.S. Dembo as follows:

> The care is detached from emotion, from use, from necessity—from everything except the most unconscionable of the emotions. And that lake which appears in the night of love seemed to me to be quite real even though it was actually fog. (CL, 168)

GUEST ROOM
*Poetry* 105: 6 (Mar. 1965). Oppen discusses this poem in a letter to JOD, assuring her that it is not an attack on her but on a life of privilege that he associates with

his West Coast family and friends during the 1920s in California:

> It isn't, not an attack on anyone who thinks of—well, understanding—
> as the purpose of one's life. The poem uses the Nassau house, but I was
> thinking of Seville and George and of San Mateo. The first part of the
> poem too: 'the noise of wealth, the clamor of wealth' is the dinner par-
> ties of San Mateo." (SL, 94)

An early draft of "Guest Room," titled "Ninth Floor," appears on the same page
as the following poem which continues the theme of class resentment:

> Overlooking
> The park,
>
> She clings
> By bibelots
> To a line          .
>
> Of descent.  She trembles
> In a way
> That would have amazed
>
> Those merchant New Yorkers
> From whom she inherits.
> (UCSD 16, 21, 12)

Giovanni's *Rape of the Sabine Women* at Wildenstein's
*Poetry* 104:2 (May 1964). Poem refers to the 16th-century sculptor Giovanni of
Bologna's statue, *Rape of the Sabine Women* (1582), currently in Loggia de'Lanzi
in Florence. Wildenstein's: an art gallery on East 64th Street in Manhattan.

A Language of New York
Omitted from CPF. Most of this poem is included and expanded in the title poem
in *Of Being Numerous* (NCP, 163–88). "I cannot even now / Altogether disen-
gage myself / From those men": Refers to Oppen's infantry experiences in France
during World War. II. "The pure products of America——": the opening line of
William Carlos Williams's poem "To Elsie," from *Spring and All* (1923). "The cap-
ital grows upon one in time . . . ": Whitman letter to his mother, April 19, 1864
(*The Collected Writings of Walt Whitman: The Correspondence*, Vol. I: 1842-1867.
Ed. Edwin Haviland Miller [New York: New York University Press, 1961], 211).
When he reprints the poem in OBN (NCP, 188) GO changes "capital" to
Whitman's spelling, "capitol."

EROS

Epigraph: II Esdra 4:45. "To the plaque of the ten thousand / Last men of the Commune": a reference to the Paris Commune and the 10,000 communards killed in 1871 (147 of whom were executed at the Père-Lachaise Cemetery). "grave / Of Largo Caballero and the monuments to the Resistance—": Largo Caballero, Spanish politician and leader of Socialist Party. He served as prime minister of the Spanish Republic, following the Popular Front victory in 1936, and lived in exile in France after Franco's victory. He survived imprisonment at Dachau during World War II and died in France, where he is buried at Père-Lachaise.

BOY'S ROOM

*Inside Outer Space: New Poems of the Space Age.* Ed. Robert Vas Dias (Garden City, NY: Doubleday/Anchor, 1970). A variant of this poem appears in a letter to William Bronk, December 21, 1962, which begins:

> It is probably tiresome
> To write of the writing
> Of poetry. But a friend
> Who saw the rooms of Keats and Shelley
> At the lake
> Saw 'they were just boys' rooms'
>
> (SL, 73)

PENOBSCOT

*Maine Lines: 101 Contemporary Poems About Maine.* Ed. Richard Aldridge (Philadelphia: Lippincott, 1970). Two early drafts suggest that the poem was a response to William Carlos Williams's version of America in "A Red Wheelbarrow," as suggested by their titles: "So Much Depends Upon" and "American Primitive" (UCSD 16, 21, 21). The Oppens often summered on Penobscot Bay in Maine, particularly on Little Deer and Eagle islands. In a letter to George Johnson, GO explained his affinity for "'that other antiquity,' the Northern, the non-classic, and I read, for example, Langland in preference to Chaucer" (SL, 187). "winter // That burns like a Tyger": Refers to Blake's "The Tyger," a poem quoted also in "Myth of the Blaze" (MB) and "The Poem" (P).

STREET

*Poetry* 104:2 (May 1964). Bergen Street is in Brooklyn, New York.

CARPENTER'S BOAT

*Agenda* 4: 3-4 (1966). Omitted from CPF.

OF THIS ALL THINGS . . .
*Chicago* (Oct. 1973). Omitted from CPF. "The girl who walked / Indian style .
. .": a reference to MO. See also "Anniversary Poem" (NCP, 225).

THE PEOPLE, THE PEOPLE
*Poetry* 105: 6 (Mar. 1965). RBDP points out that in notes for a reading of "The
People, the People" at the Guggenheim Museum, GO indicates that the poem
"concerns the possible disappearance of the radical intellectual, and that it derives
from his reading of Norman Mailer's novel *Barbary Shore*. The 'she' of the poem
is related to the character [in the novel] of Guinevere; in both novel and poem
she is 'the people'" (SL, 421, n. 24).

BAHAMAS
*Ironwood* 9 (1977). Omitted from CPF. The Oppens were in Nassau with JOD
from December 1964 until March 1965.

THE FOUNDER
*Agenda* 4:3-4 (1966).

PRIMITIVE
*Poetry* 104:2 (May 1964).

ALPINE
*Elizabeth* XIII (July 1969). Title poem of A.

RATIONALITY
"that 'part // of consciousness' . . . " Appears also in "Debt" (CP, 39).

NIGHT SCENE
Omitted from CPF.

THE MAYAN GROUND
Opening passage, from *The Book of the Jaguar Priest: A translation of the book of
Chilam Balam of Tizimin*. Trans. Maud Worcester Makemson. (New York: Henry
Schuman, 1951.) "The poet wrote of that we try to break": Refers to Denise
Levertov's poem "Matins" from *The Jacob's Ladder*:

> the real, the new-laid
> egg whose speckled shell
> the poet fondles and must break
> if he will be nourished.

Denise Levertov, *The Jacob's Ladder* (New York: New Directions, 1961), 58).

These lines are also quoted in GO's essay, "The Mind's Own Place" (*Montemora* 1 [Fall 1975]: 134.

QUOTATIONS
*The New Naked Poetry: Recent American Poetry in Open Forms.* Eds. Stephen Berg and Robert Mezey (Indianapolis: Bobbs-Merrill, 1976).

RED HOOK: DECEMBER
Red Hook: a neighborhood in Brooklyn near to where the Oppens lived during the early 1960s.

THE BICYCLES AND THE APEX
Originally written as prose (UCSD 16, 21, 33). "Van Gogh went hungry and what shoe salesman / Does not envy him now?": Among Van Gogh's most famous early paintings is a series of peasant shoes. John Birch Societies: a reference to the anti-Communist political group of the 1950s and 1960s.

THE OCCURRENCES
Not the same as "The Occurrences" in SNE (NCP, 212).

MONUMENT
"the Norman chapel . . . " "the armed man . . . ": reference to the Abbey of St. Michel in Normandy, northern France. The Oppens visited it in the early 1930s, and MO describes the trip in ML, 134. "[T]he armed man" and "The great sword" refer to the statue of the Archangel St. Michel, as described in Henry Adams's *Mont St. Michel and Chartres*, which GO had read.

NIECE
Refers to Diane ("Andy") Meyer, Oppen's niece and the daughter of his sister Elizabeth (Libby), who died in 1960.

THE BUILDING OF THE SKYSCRAPER
*The Nation* (Dec. 14, 1964). *The Gift Outright: America to Her Poets.* Ed. Helen Plotz (New York: Greenwillow/ William Morrow, 1977).

A NARRATIVE
*Paris Review* 33 (Winter-Spring 1965). Originally titled "To——," the dedication possibly to his sister JOD (see SL, 89), although RBDP thinks that the effaced name could also be that of Denise Levertov. See SL, 383. "The blind man / Knew": The

"blind man" refers to John Milton. "His mind / Is its own place": Variation on Milton's lines from Paradise Lost I, lines 250-55:

> Hail horrors, hail
> Infernal world, and thou profoundest Hell
> Receive thy new Possessor: One who brings
> A mind not to be chang'd by Place or Time.
> The mind is its own place, and in itself
> Can make a Heav'n of Hell, a Hell of Heav'n.

The phrase "the mind's own place" is the title of an essay by Oppen. Atlantic Avenue is in Brooklyn, New York. David McAleavey conjectures that the reference to William Bronk is to his poem "The Nature of the Universe" (*The World, the Worldless* [New York: New Directions-San Francisco Review, 1964], 43):

> we
> are the inner mirror of those stars, who find
> only an ecstasy to outfeel
> horror . . .

Quoted in David McAleavey, "Unrolling Universe: A Reading of Oppen's *This in Which*." *Paideuma* 10:1 (Spring 1981): 105-28.

PRO NOBIS
*Chicago* (Oct. 1973). Pro Nobis: "for us" (Latin). From the Catholic prayer: *Ave Maria, Mater Dei, ora pro nobis peccatoribus, nunc, et in hora mortis nostrae* (*Holy Mary, mother of God, pray for us sinners now, and in the hour of our death*). In a letter to George Johnston, GO says, "To begin with, the catastrophe of human lives in the 'thirties which seemed to me to put poetry and the purposes of poetry in question——I wrote of that in a poem called Pro Nobis. But, later, that we had a daughter. And still hesitate over a line, thinking of my daughter reading it . . . " (SL, 186).

TO C.T.
As the epigraph indicates, C.T. is the British poet Charles Tomlinson. The poem is a versification of a letter that Oppen sent to him, April 29, 1963 (SL, 383, n. 10).

# OF BEING NUMEROUS (1968)

*Of Being Numerous* is George Oppen's best-known book, having won the Pulitzer Prize in Poetry in 1969. The title refers to Oppen's lifelong concern with unity in diversity, with achieving autonomy while living among others. In the title poem, the problem is expressed as "the shipwreck of the singular" represented by Robinson Crusoe on his island. GO asks how is it possible to retain agency when "[we] are pressed, pressed on each other." This was the dilemma that faced him when he decided to give up poetry during the 1930s, feeling he could not instrumentalize his poetry by making it serve social goals. This same dilemma faced him again when he took up poetry in the late 1950s and increased during the period of the Vietnam War. This latter crisis provides the occasion for numerous poems in the book, as GO attempted to negotiate his older Marxist views against the claims of the New Left and youth movements.

Oppen's relationship to the New Left is a complex one to which he returns often in subsequent poems and letters. To be "numerous" in the tradition of the Old Left was to generalize individuals around common categories of class affiliation (the proletariat, the Party) rather than express localized demands and desires. Speaking of the liberal humanist tradition, Oppen says, "Well, it's been tried . . . We've SEEN it fail in our own lifetimes Because really each one has his own life—the historical factor is IN his own life or it is nowhere" (SL, 190). The New Left, on the other hand, "despite any lapse of logic has had unchallengeable authority in that its people spoke for themselves . . . They said what they wanted——" (SL,192). In many letters of the late 1960s, GO describes the failure of liberal traditions and expresses respect for individuals in the civil rights (and later Black Power) and anti-war movements who speak less for "the masses" than for "themselves." This fact becomes one of the meanings of being numerous.

As an artist, the crisis "of being numerous" haunts all of Oppen's work, as he strives to locate the "lyric valuables" that endure against the lure of material options and managed opinions. But on a more personal level, Oppen is signaling the value of friends and family whose comments from letters and conversations have sustained him and which are interspersed throughout the book. This conversational quality is announced from the outset. Oppen dedicated the book to his wife, Mary, "whose words in this book are entangled / inextricably among my own," a dedication which he repeated in the opening to CP as well as CPF. Her words are joined to those of other friends and family members—RBDP, Andy Meyer, John Crawford, David Antin, LO, Steven Schneider—whose words are scattered throughout the book. Oppen also quotes extensively from other writers—Heidegger, Kierkegaard, Blake, Wittgenstein—usually via inverted commas, but often as not without any citational marks (in a note found among his papers,

GO asserted that his quotes "are not allusions; they are thefts"). The book's inter-textuality is complicated by the fact that Oppen includes lines, words, and whole poems from his own previous books. His long sequence "A Language of New York," from *This in Which*, reappears in expanded form as the title poem, "Of Being Numerous." References to *Discrete Series* and other earlier volumes occur throughout. Thus the book embodies a social ethos in which the poem is creat-ed out of conversations with others—including the poet himself.

OF BEING NUMEROUS
The title poem incorporates or reworks the sequence, "A Language of New York," published in TW (NCP, 114–19).
1. "There are things / We live among . . . "
    *Maps* 2 (May 1967). "'and to see them / Is to know ourselves'.": According to a series of notes found among his papers, GO drew these lines from Robert S. Brumbaugh, *Plato for the Modern Age* (New York: Crowell-Collier, 1962). The prose quotation that concludes the poem is from MO speaking about French poet Yves Bonnefoy. In a letter to Steven Schneider of 1966, Oppen says "the next words, beyond what I've quoted, were 'that's what Douve is about,'" a reference to Bonnefoy's book *Du mouvement et de l'immobilité de Douve,* which Schneider had translated (SL, 129). The image of the salamander comes from Bonnefoy's book.
2. "So spoke of the existence of things"
    Variant of poem 1, "A Language of New York" (NCP, 114). According to a note found among his papers, Oppen based this poem on a letter from David Antin.
3. "The emotions are engaged / Entering the city"
    *Chicago* (Oct. 1973).
5. "The great stone/ Above the river"
    *Chicago* (Oct. 1973). "The great stone/ Above the river": A reference to the Brooklyn Bridge whose pylons were completed in 1875. "Which has nothing to gain, which awaits nothing": Quoted in a letter to Jane Cooper, February 12, 1974 (SL, 294).
6. "We are pressed, pressed on each other"
    "Crusoe / We say was / 'Rescued'": Robinson Crusoe's shipwreck and iso-lation provide a sustained metaphor for the human condition in this book, a motif that appears in numerous poems. Randolph Chilton describes Crusoe's rescue as follows:

> Crusoe is rescued *from* solitude *to* society, in other words, and simply by calling it a rescue, we make a social commitment. . . . Numerosity and sin-gularity give each other meaning. We need a sense of collective existence to provide the context for a sense of our own reality. (GOMP, 98-99)

7. "Obsessed, bewildered . . ."
*Chicago* (Oct. 1973). *A Brooklyn Bridge poetry walk.* Ed. Daniela Gioseffi (Brooklyn, NY: Print Center, 1972).
8. "*Amor fati*"

> *Amor fati*: Love of fate. Taken from Nietzsche, *Ecce Homo*:
> My formula for greatness in a human being is *amor fati*, that one wants nothing to be different, not forward, not backward, not in all eternity. Not merely bear what is necessary, still less conceal it—all idealism is mendaciousness in the face of what is necessary—but *love* it (Friedrich Nietzsche, *On the Genealogy of Morals, Ecce Homo*. Ed. Walter Kauffmann [NY: Random/Vintage, 1969], 258).

Early drafts of this section link the theme of fate and shipwreck to the Vietnam War:

> 'yet I do love a kind of light and a kind of voice'

> The obvious light.

> To be unable to watch
> Is to be destroyed.

> We wake in nightmare of the captured, the tortured
> and those under the planes
> Burning in napalm in the one flame of their village . . .
> The children also, the children also . .

> In meaningless open day

> Amor fati

> Dead end
> Dead end, the island

> The absolute singular

> The unearthly bonds
> Of the singular
> Which is the bright light of shipwreck

> (UCSD 16, 22, 9)

9. "'Whether, as the intensity of seeing increases . . .'"
Opening lines refer to 1965 letter sent by RBDP to GO regarding an early draft of *Of Being Numerous*. In her letter RBDP had queried "Whether, as the intensity of seeing increases, one's distance from Them, the people, does not also

increase." (SL, 390, n. 23) RBDP had suggested dropping section 7, to which GO responded, "I don't agree really. I need that, and need it as flat as it is to establish that half of the burden of the poem which is hardest to establish—the concepts evolved from the fact of being numerous, without which we are marooned, ship-wrecked—it is in fact unthinkable without them" (SL, 121). In a 1968 letter to William Bronk GO remembers RBDP's line, now in relationship to student protests at Columbia University with which she was involved:

A young friend 'phoned during the first hour of the Columbia sit-in. She talked for—I think—more than half an hour. Troubled by events and the difficulty of finding her role, her place. She wanted to be among the *actives*—and felt that she somehow was not and could not wholly be so——Talked, as I say, a long time. After she hung up I remembered that it was from one of her letters to me that I took the quotation in *Numerous*

'Whether, as the intensity of seeing increases, one's distance

from Them, the People, does not also increase'

Dramatic. She had somehow foreseen it. (SL, 176)

10. "Or, in that light, New arts! Dithyrambic . . ."

*Chicago* (Oct. 1973). "Dithyrambic, audience-as-artists" presumably refers to the youth revolt as well as the Brechtian happenings and living theater in late 1960s art world.

11. "it is *that* light"

*Chicago* (Oct. 1973). "Phyllis——not neo-classic" alludes to William Carlos Williams's Phyllis and Corydon in the Idyl of *Paterson* IV.

12. "'In these explanations it is presumed . . . '"

According to Burton Hatlen, the opening quotation is from Alfred North Whitehead, *Process and Reality*, although GO (in a note on the series mentioned above with regard to #1) indicates that it derives from Pierre Teilhard de Chardin. See Burton Hatlen, "Opening up the Text: George Oppen's 'Of Being Numerous,'" *Ironwood* 26, Vol. 13:2 (1985): 263-95. "They were patient/ With the world": An early draft of this section ("Quoted from Carlyle's *Goethe*") changes these lines to "We are patient with the world" and places them in quotation marks, suggesting they are derived from Carlyle's essay, published in 1828.

13. "unable to begin / At the beginning"

Variant of poem 2, "A Language of New York" (NCP, 114).

14. "I cannot even now / Altogether disengage myself"

Variant of poem 3, "A Language of New York" (NCP, 115).

15. "Chorus (androgynous): 'Find me / So that I will exist . . . '"

Oppen quotes most of this poem and comments on it in a letter to Diane Wakoski of February-March 1965: "and yet I would say: 'I, IIII, find me, find my navel, so that it will exist, find my nipples, so they will exist, find every hair of my belly, find . . . ' It is a root of poetry, it is indeed . . . Because it seems to me still the pitfall that has trapped every woman poet who has written in English: I am good (or I am bad); find me" (CL, 110).

16. "' . . . he who will not work shall not eat'"

The poem is a setting of the opening to Kierkegaard's *Fear and Trembling*: Between the ellipsis at the penultimate line and the conclusion is the following passage (translation differs slightly from Oppen's):

> He who will not work does not get the bread but remains deluded, as the gods deluded Orpheus with an airy figure in place of the loved one, deluded him because he was effeminate, not courageous, because he was a cithara-player, not a man. Here it is of no use to have Abraham for one's father, nor to have seventeen ancestors—he who will not work must take note of what is written about the maidens of Israel, for he gives birth to wind, but he who is willing to work gives birth to his own father. (Søren Kierkegaard, *Fear and Trembling and the Sickness Unto Death*. Trans. Walter Lowrie [Princeton: Princeton University Press, 1954], 38).

According to Henry Weinfield, Oppen relied on the 1939 Robert Payne translation of *Fear and Trembling* (London: Oxford University Press, 1939), 29-30. Henry Weinfield, "'Because the Known and the Unknown Touch': The Music of Thought in George Oppen's 'Of Being Numerous'" (Unpublished MS).

18. "It is the air of atrocity"

An early draft of this poem is included in a letter to Steven Schneider, prefaced by the remark "I wrote this, just into a note book. I don't mean it's poetry:" (UCSD 16, 22, 17)

19. "Now in the helicopters the casual will"

"The fly in the bottle": a phrase used by Wittgenstein in *The Philosophical Investigations*, #309: "What is your aim in philosophy?—To shew the fly the way out of the fly-bottle" (Ludwig Wittgenstein, *The Philosophical Investigations*. Trans. G.E.M. Anscombe [New York: Macmillan, 1953], 103e). Oppen links this remark to President Lyndon Johnson's role in the escalating Vietnam War and the use of helicopters in that war. In a letter to Alex Mourelatos, Oppen says

> I think of the phrase 'the fly in the bottle' as a quotation from you, not as a quotation from Wit[tgenstein] because that was the moment when we understood each other . . . So—a quotation from you. And in the context of the poem, immediately the vision of the insane, poisonous Johnsonian flies . . . (SL, 177)

20. "—They await"

*Chicago* (Oct. 1973). The poem was originally part of letter to Andy Meyer (UCSD: 16, 22, 19). "Hardy's poem of Christmas": Thomas Hardy's "The Oxen," written in 1915 during World War I, concludes with the following lines:

> So fair a fancy few would weave
> In these years! Yet, I feel,

If someone said on Christmas Eve,
"Come; see the oxen kneel,

"In the lonely barton by yonder coomb
Our childhood used to know,"
I should go with him in the gloom,
Hoping it might be so.
(Thomas Hardy, *Collected Poems* [New York: Macmillan, 1952], 439.)

21. "There can be a brick"

*Chicago* (Oct. 1973). Appears as poem 6 in "A Language of New York" (NCP, 117). "Here is the brick, it was waiting . . . " Quoted in letter to Aubrey Degnan-Sutter (October 1964): "I believe we can't be astonished by any hallucination whatever. Whereas we are totally astonished by daylight, by any brick in a brick wall we focus on" (SL, 105).

23. "'Half free / And half mad'"

"The Mustang": a reference to the Ford car, introduced in the late 1960s.

24. "In this nation"

*The Gift Outright: America to Her Poets*, ed. Helen Plotz (New York: Morrow, 1977). "Covenant!" The New England Puritans believed that they were under a direct mandate from God to form a New Jerusalem in the new world. They found doctrinal support for this idea in the Covenant made with Abraham (and ratified with the birth of Christ) to deliver the chosen people of Israel which, they felt, could be extended to the first settlers of New England.

25. "Strange that the youngest people I know"

Appears as poem 7 of "A Language of New York" (NCP, 118). "'The pure products of America'——" refers to William Carlos Williams, section XVIII of *Spring and All* (also called "To Elsie"), whose opening stanza reads: "The pure products of America / go crazy— / mountain folk from Kentucky."

26. "They carry nativeness / To a conclusion"

"How shall one know a generation . . . " Quoted in a letter to JOD, ca. 1964–1965:

To recognize the new, the 'new generation':
not by the dew on them. On the contrary, where there are the clearest
and sharpest marks of trampling, of devastation, destitution, the rawest
wounds, is the head of the army column. (SL, 109)

27. "It is difficult now to speak of poetry—"

*Maps* 2 (May 1967). *The New Naked Poetry: Recent American Poetry in Open Forms*. Eds. Stephen Berg and Robert Mezey (Indianapolis: Bobbs-Merrill, 1976). *Mark in Time: Portraits & Poetry / San Francisco*. Ed. Nick Harvey (San Francisco: Glide Publications, 1971).

34. "Like the wind in the trees and the bells"

*Chicago* (Oct. 1973). *Maps* 2 (May 1967). "'. . . a Female Will to hide the most evident God / Under a covert . . . ' " From William Blake, *Jerusalem*, Ch. 2, plate 34, line 32:

> This, woman has claimed as her own & man is no more,
> Albion is the tabernacle of Vala & her temple,
> And not the Tabernacle & Temple of the Most High!
> O Albion, why wilt thou create a female will,
> To hide the most evident God in a hidden covert, even
> In the shadows of a woman & a secluded Holy Place
> (William Blake, *The Poems of William Blake*. Ed. W.H. Stevenson
> [London: Longman, 1971], 685.)

37. " ' . . . approached the window as if to see . . . ' "

Opening line taken from Henry James's story, " The Story in It." See note to opening poem of DS, "The knowledge not of sorrow, you were / saying . . . " "The boredom which disclosed / Everything— // I should have written" refers to subsequent lines in the same poem concerning Heidegger's concept of boredom as defined in his acceptance speech upon assuming the Chair of Philosophy at the University of Freiburg in 1929. See interview in CL (169) and Edward Hirsch in GOMP (172-73).

40. "The capitol grows upon one in time . . . "

Appears as poem 8 in "A Language of New York" (NCP, 119) where "capitol" is spelled "capital." See note, NCP, 375. In a letter to John Crawford, Oppen explains the conclusion of "Of Being Numerous":

> There is an almost audible click in the brain to mark the transition
> between thought which is available because it has already been thought,
> and the thinking of the single man, the thinking of a man as if he were
> a single man . . . "Of Being Numerous" is constructed around that click,
> of course—and the poem ends with the word "curious." I had set myself
> once before to say forthrightly "We want to be here" [NCP, 159], and
> the long poem ends almost jokingly with "curious." But it is not a joke
> entirely. If I were asked, Why do we want to be here—I would say: it is
> curious——the thing is curious——" (SL, 402, n. 6)

HISTORIC PUN
*Poetry* 111:3 (1967). "La petite vie": Fr., "The little life." Sacré-Coeur: the Basilica of Sacré-Coeur, which offers an extensive view south over Paris. Buttes Chaumont: a park in the Belleville district of Paris.

A KIND OF GARDEN: A POEM FOR MY SISTER
Dedicated to GO's sister, JOD, the editor of San Francisco Review editions and close friend and confidante throughout the poet's life.

ROUTE

*Grosseteste Review* 6: 1-4 (1973). *Open Poetry: Four Anthologies of Expanded Poems.* Eds. Ronald Gross and George Quasha, *et al.* (New York: Simon & Schuster, 1973). Based on letters to various correspondents, it would appear that the poem was well underway as of 1966. See the letter to John Crawford which quotes the phrase, "Words cannot be wholly transparent," from section 4 (SL, 144). *Wen Fu* of Lu Chi: a third-century A.D. treatise on the art of writing by Lu Chi (261-303 A.D.).

1. "Tell the beads of the chromosomes like a rosary"

"Love in the genes, if it fails": In a letter to John Crawford of 1973, Oppen advises, "Read Langland 'for truth telleth that love is a treacle that abateth sin' to me, – the line moved me tremendously—meaning to me what I wrote so much later : ['love in the genes—if it fails . . . ' " (SL, 254). The passage quoted by Oppen is in the section of *Piers Plowman* called "The Vision of Holy Church." In the C-text original, the lines read as follows:

> For treuthe telleth that loue ys tryacle for synne,
> And most souereyne salue for saule and for body. (Passus I, 147-48)
> (William Langland, *The Vision of William Concerning Piers the*
> *Plowman,* Vol. I. Ed. Walter W. Skeat [London: Oxford University Press,
> 1968], 33.)

3. "Not to reduce the thing to nothing——"

"We will produce no sane man again": Quoted in a letter to Stephen Schneider:

> that a morality is possible within a family. It is, as you say, 'in the chro-
> mosomes'. It can make an area of human life possible. If it disappears,
> we will produce no sane people again. (UCSD 16, 22, 17)

4. "Words cannot be wholly transparent."

"The sea anemone dreamed of something . . . " In a draft of the poem, Oppen adds a note: "an inconceivably brutal universe; it is possible that sea anemones dream continually." For a discussion of this section and the draft see Michael Davidson, "Palimtexts" in *Ghostlier Demarcations: Modern Poetry and the Material Word* (Berkeley: University of California Press, 1997), 74-75. "Nothing more real than boredom": one of numerous references to Heidegger's idea of boredom as defined in his 1929 inaugural lecture upon assuming the Chair of Philosophy at Freiburg. See Eric Mottram, "The Political Responsibilities of the Poet" (GOMP, 151).

5. "In Alsace, during the war . . . "

On story of Pierre Adam, see CL interview, pp. 170-72.

8. "Cars on the highway"

"The wheels of the overturned wreck . . . ": GO was involved in a car acci-
dent in 1925 in which a passenger was killed. Cf. SL, xi. In a letter to John
Crawford, GO quotes this section (titled "Route") and explains:

> I'd written it—with levity—for David Antin and his [wife] Ely [Eleanor
> Antin]——not TOO much coincidence that your car flipped a couple
> of months later, since cars do flip . . . If I am making any point for your
> comfort, I mean we all know, I mean me too, we all just barely make it.
> (UCSD 16, 22, 49)

10. "Not the symbol but the scene this pavement leads . . ."
"Virgin / what was there to be thought": A version of the St. John of the Cross
poem, "*Del Verbo Divino.*" MO's translation of the poem is as follows:

> what is *there*     to be thought
>
>
> comes by the road
> if you will give it shelter
>
>
> Mary Oppen, *Poems & Transpositions* (New York: Montemora
> Foundation, 1980), n.p.

The original poem reads as follows:

> Del Verbo divino
> La Virgen prenada
> Viene de camino
> Si le dais posada.
>
>
> Pregnant with the holy
> word will come the Virgin
> walking down the road
> if you will take her in."
> (*The Poems of St. John of the Cross.* Trans. Willis Barnstone
> [Bloomington: Indiana University Press, 1968], 94.)

11. "Tell the life of the mind . . . "
"Of it, the word it . . . ": According to RBDP, this is a response to Robert
Duncan's preface to *Bending the Bow*, published in 1968, which refers to the word
"it":

> for It has only the actual universe in which to realize Itself. We ourselves
> in our actuality, as the poem in its actuality, its thingness, are facts, factors,
> in which It makes Itself real. Having only these actual words, these actu-
> al imaginations that come to us as we work." Robert Duncan, *Bending
> the Bow* (New York: New Directions, 1968), vii.

12. "To insist that what is true is good . . . "
"That tree / whose fruit": A variation on the opening lines of Milton's
*Paradise Lost*: "Of Man's First Disobedience, and the Fruit / Of that Forbidden

Tree . . ."

13. "Department of plants and Structures . . . "

Eric Mottram describes a 1973 reading in London where Oppen interpolated a line between the last two:

'Substance itself which is the subject of all our planning'
*and our most profound companionships*
And by this we are carried into the incalculable
(GOMP, 165)

The quoted line comes from Heidegger's *Essays on Metaphysics: Identity and Difference* (New York: Philosophical Library, 1960). In a "note to himself" which appears in SL, GO describes the process by which the line "Substance itself which is the subject of all our planning" was derived from his reading of Heidegger's book:

I knew I was envious of the phrase; it occurred to me that where Heidegger had used the word substance, I would probably not have thought of it, and would have used the clumsy word 'matter.' And I wrote 'which is the subject of our planning' with the knowledge that it was my own phrase, an alteration of his, but derived from some other sentence in his essay. (SL, 135)

14. "There was no other guarantee . . . " "Ours aren't the only madmen tho they have burned thousands of men and women alive . . . ": Probably a reference to the U. S. policy of dropping napalm from helicopters on Vietnam. Cf. letter to JOD of 1966:

To try to write it down bluntly, I mean that the Vietnamese—a great many of them—are going to be burnt alive, and a great many subjected to various careful tortures—and we will, in a way, accept it, we will talk politics, and try to find Johnson and the CIA a way out in order not to be taken into a general war and the end of us. (SL, 130)

Cabeza de Vaca: Álvar Núñez Cabeza de Vaca (ca.1490–ca. 1557). Spanish explorer shipwrecked near Galveston, Texas, in 1528, set off with three other men toward Mexico and for eight years wandered the Gulf Coast, occasionally taken into captivity by Indian tribes. His group survived potential hostilities by assuming roles as shamans and medicine men and gained a reputation among native peoples for performing miracles. Hernán Cortés (1485–1547): Spanish nobleman and explorer who with a small group of followers attacked and conquered the Aztec city of Tenochtitlán, building Mexico City out of its ruin.

A THEOLOGICAL DEFINITION

*Poetry* 111:3 (1967). *Our Own Thing: Contemporary Thought in Poetry.* Ed. Gretchen Crafts (Englewood Cliffs, NJ: Prentice-Hall, 1973).

POWER, THE ENCHANTED WORLD

". . . *That come before the swallow dares . . .*": from Shakespeare, *The Winter's Tale* (Act

IV, Scene iv): "daffodils, / That come before the swallow dares, and take / The winds of March with beauty."

BALLAD
*Poetry* 111:3 (1967). Swan's Island: in Penobscot Bay, Maine, where the Oppens often sailed.

# SEASCAPE: NEEDLE'S EYE (1972)

Published in 1972, *Seascape: Needle's Eye* was the first book since *Discrete Series* not published by New Directions. After being withdrawn from publication by another small press, it was published by the Sumac Press in Fremont, Michigan. It appeared at a moment when Oppen was beginning to receive some national and international attention, following his receipt of the Pulitzer Prize in 1969 for *Of Being Numerous*.

A large portion of *Seascape* (whose original title was "Horizon: Needle's Eye") concerns the San Francisco Bay area to which the Oppens moved in 1966 and where they were to live until GO's death. He had grown up in San Francisco, and this return provoked a series of reflections on a landscape that was haunted with past family and social history. The poems in the volume deal with weather, geography, and the built environment of the West, issues that differentiate this volume from previous books. These themes are not only geographical but political, as GO meditates on the youth culture of the late 1960s, viewed through the Haight Ashbery hippie movement and culminating in the Rolling Stones concert at Altamont Pass which the Oppens attended.

"Seascape: Needle's Eye" is titled "Of the Needle's Eye: 1968–1969" in CPF and differs significantly from CP. The contents are as follows:

Rock Festival, Altamont, California [opening to "Some San Francisco
    Poems"]
A Barbarity [variant of "The Book of Job . . . " in *Myth of the Blaze*]
Some San Francisco Poems
A Morality Play: Preface
'And their Winter and Night in Disguise'
Anniversary Poem
The Translucent Mechanics
Of the Needle's Eye [variant of section 6 of SNE]
The Taste
The Impossible Poem

But So As By Fire
The Song [variant of "Song, the Winds of Downhill"]

Dedication. The original edition (but not CP) featured the dedication "for Linda," MO and GO's daughter, who was living in Austin, Texas.

FROM A PHRASE OF SIMONE WEIL'S AND SOME WORDS OF HEGEL'S
*Grosseteste Review* 6:1-4 (1973). *Red Cedar Review* 8:2-3 (Dec. 1973). Although the specific phrase of Simone Weil that inspired the poem has not been identified, one may assume that it comes from her book *Attente de Dieu* (*Waiting for God*), from which the image of the "needle's eye" is derived. See note for "Of Hours" below. "the outer / Limit of the ego." In a manuscript draft, this phrase appears as follows:

> The burden of isolation and egotism
> Intellect: the extreme outer limit of the ego
>
> The tree remains a tree, and in fact a willow, just as it was,
> but it has become a dream, all happening of itself
> (UCSD 16, 23, 2)

"Ob via      the obvious": Oppen's play on the Latin derivation of obvious meaning "in the way, in the street." See John Peck in GOMP, 68.

THE OCCURRENCES
Not the same as the poem by same title in TW. "Toys of the children wings / Of the wasp": Possible reference to Pound's wasp in the *Pisan Cantos* and mentioned by GO in his CL interview: "Just about the time I'm beginning to consider Pound an idiot, I come to something like the little wasp in the *Pisan Cantos*, and I know that I'm reading a very great poet" (CL, 170).

ANIMULA
Epigraph: *animula blandula vagula* ( "little pleasant soul wandering"): a variation on Hadrian's address to the soul, as it appears in Aelius Spartianus's *Life of Hadrian* (chapter 25, section 9). Oppen reverses the second two terms:

> Animula vagula blandula,
> hospes comesque corporis,
> quae nunc abibis in loca
> pallidula rigida nudula

Byron translated the fragment in "Adrian's Address to His Soul, When Dying" as follows:

> Ah! gentle, fleeting, wav'ring sprite,
> Friend and associate of this clay!
> To what unknown region borne,
> Wilt thou, now, wing thy distant flight?
> No more, with wonted humour gay,
> But pallid, cheerless, and forlorn.

George Gordon Byron, *Complete Poetical Works,* Vol. 1. Ed. Jerome McGann (New York: Oxford: Clarendon Press, 1980), 69-70.

"Comes down the road": from St. John of the Cross, "*Del Verbo Divino.*" See note to "Route."

WEST

*Grosseteste Review* 6: 1-4 (1973). In early drafts titled "The Dream Under the Hill," a phrase that is reminiscent of Robert Duncan's poem, "Often I Am Permitted to Return to a Meadow," from *Opening of the Field* (New York: Grove, 1960), 7. Remarks in italics are taken from a letter to GO from Andy Meyer, undated:

> I think more of those people in the woods waiting to go waiting to go to Japan. It costs nothing to live. What will their children say of them, "my parents waited in the woods." What did the children of this generation say, "My father trod a path to work every day. I don't know what he did. We weren't hungry. My mother stayed home, sometimes we went to the country." (UCSD 16, 7, 26)

Writing to Michael Heller in 1972, Oppen uses "West" to describe *Seascape* in general:

> Needle's Eye: I think you say correctly, speak accurately of some change in the language    the language 'rises' a little? etherealizes a lit-tle, so imminently confronted by one's temporality——even a camel might peek thru at that point, a camel or an old gent——
> 'in nakedness / inseparable' I meant: it coheres,    it coheres *of itself.* (SL, 249)

OF HOURS

*Sumac* 3:2 (Winter 1971). Title in *Sumac* is "Book of Hours." "as if a nail whose wide head / were time and space": from Simone Weil, *Waiting for God.* Weil refers to affliction as a "nail whose point is applied at the very center of the soul, whose head is all necessity spreading throughout space and time." Simone Weil, *Waiting For God* (trans. Emma Craufurd [New York: Putnam, 1951], 34-35). GO discusses this passage in his interview with Kevin Power (*Montemora* 4), as does John Peck in GOMP, 68. "Old friend    old poet": a reference to Ezra Pound, with whom Oppen was reunited briefly in 1969, an incident described in his interview with Burton Hatlen and Tom Mandel (GOMP, 26-28). Oppen is responding to Pound's anti-Semitism and his support of Mussolini during the war by invoking his own experience "Burying my dogtag with H / For Hebrew in the rubble of Alsace." The question to the "old poet," "What is it you 'loved' / Twisting your voice    your walk" refers to Pound's lines in Canto LXXXI:

> What thou lovest well remains,
>
>                              the rest is dross
> What thou lov'st well shall not be reft from thee
> What thou lov'st well is thy true heritage

> Ezra Pound, *The Cantos of Ezra Pound* (New York: New Directions, 1986), 534-35.

"Fought ice // Fought shifting stones . . . Fought / No man" resembles Pound's reference in Canto LXXIV to Odysseus as "no man" ( "I am noman, my name is noman") when confronting the Cyclops in *Odyssey* IX, 366. "what was that rage // Before Leger's art poster / In war time Paris . . . " MO in ML describes a furlough that Oppen spent in Paris during World War II:

> George walked through Paris to the Boulevards, where he looked on, incredulous, at the Boulevardiers, who, momentarily safe behind Allied front lines, sipped ersatz coffee and nibbled delicacies concocted of sawdust; as they daintily continued their café lives, on the kiosk were large beautiful, extravagant posters advertising Leger's latest exhibit. George says, "I nearly went berserk; there was no way to express my anger at these Parisians who could care about such mediocrity at such a time." (ML, 177)

SONG, THE WINDS OF DOWNHILL
"'out of poverty / to begin // again'": from Charles Simic, *White*:

> Out of poverty
> to begin again:
>
> quick.

Speak and then wait,
As if this light

Will continue to linger
On the threshold.

Charles Simic, *White* (New York: New Rivers Press, 1972).
Portions of this poem appeared as "The Song" in A and CPF (see "Uncollected
Published Poems," NCP 299).

SOME SAN FRANCISCO POEMS
This sequence was originally titled, "For Robert Duncan" (UCSD 16, 23, 10).
1. *"Moving over the hills, crossing the irrigation / canals"*
GO and MO attended the 1969 Altamont Speedway Free Festival near
Livermore in Contra Costa County which featured a performance by the Rolling
Stones. Reference to the *"Needle's eye"* is linked to the image of the nail, as
defined by Simone Weil (see note for "Of Hours" above). In his *Ironwood* 5 inter-
view with David Gitin, Oppen comments on this image:

> It is true what I wrote there, 'over the wonderful hills the young people
> walking somewhat disgruntled.' It was necessary to park one's car and
> walk a mile. Nobody looked at my wife and me, and people had, what
> the poem says, before the music started, everyone turned very sharply
> into himself or herself. Kind of a masturbatory atmosphere. Banging
> upon the spike was pretty literal. I gave it the title "Image: Of the
> Needle's Eye." That "needle's eye, needle's eye" is all through the series.
> It at times simply means the horizon, the silver horizon, water on the
> bottom sky" (David Gitin, "A Conversation with George Oppen."
> *Ironwood* 5. 3:1 [1975]: 22).

In his interview with Kevin Power, Oppen explains that "the remark about 'their
long hair they seem / to be in mourning' was an observation not an advance
response. We didn't know anything about the murder [of a concertgoer by Hell's
Angels bodyguards] then." *Montemora* 4 (1978): 202.
2. A Morality Play: Preface
*Grosseteste Review* 6: 1-4 (1973). *Stony Brook* 3-4 (1969). *Jewish-American
Literature: An Anthology*. Ed. Abraham Chapman (New York: Mentor/New
American Library, 1974). *Nothing Doing in London* 2 (Jan. 1968). "A city street /
Leads to the bay": Polk Street, where the Oppens lived in San Francisco, *does* lead
directly to the San Francisco Bay, ending at Ghirardelli Square on the waterfront.
"Tamalpais in cloud": a mountain in Marin County visible throughout the Bay
area. An early draft of the poem presents a considerably different version:

to begin:    Within the Golden Gate

Which is the least golden
And among the great entrances of the world

Are groups and tracts of homes
On the hills
And the coves of the bay

Places unrecorded
Their names have no history

Like the breezy young women
And their presumed 'affairs'

And the complacent little center
Of the city

We have lived beyond the public theory, the wind

At every summit

Nothing is opaque

Nor was Eden

You will see the young couples
Leaving again in rags

(UCSD 16, 23, 12)

The version published in *Nothing Doing in London* links the morality play motif
with Objectivism. Following the lines, "Tamalpais in cloud," GO writes:

One is concious also of the farmlands

Place names unrecorded      local knowledge
Of the heavy hills

It is not that one means to bring home
A moral to an audience

We are those selfish travelers
Happiest in foreign streets

Insomuch as we are not travelers
We are afraid

Courage of the traveler
Piety

We said
*Objectivist*
3. 'And Their Winter and Night in Disguise'

    *Grosseteste Review* 6: 1-4 (1973). *Stony Brook* 3-4 (1969). *Jewish-American Literature: An Anthology*. Ed. Abraham Chapman (New York: Mentor/New American Library, 1974). *Calafia: The California Poetry*. Ed. Ishmael Reed (Berkeley:Y'Bird Books, 1979).Title derived from William Blake, "Nurses's Song," from his *Songs of Experience*:

        Your spring & your day are wasted in play
        And your winter and night in disguise.

See also SL, 302. Irving Younger was assistant district attorney in New York City and someone with whom Oppen corresponded on several occasions. His article in *The Nation* (Aug. 14, 1967) is entitled "Pornography and Violence" and concerns the legal implications of censorship. The passage preceding that quoted by GO reads as follows: "Who has not then said to himself, 'if I could buy normalcy for that [disabled] child at the price of my sight (or my right arm, or both my legs, or my life), I would pay it.' So with artists . . . " (124). "a crescent strip of beach": a reference to Pedro Point, a beach south of San Francisco on Highway 1. When asked about the location by the editor, GO said that it was the place where the coast commuter bus line ended. GO and MO would take the bus to the end of the line, get out, and walk on the beach. After Pedros Point, Highway 1 climbs steeply to traverse high cliffs above the Pacific Ocean. Hence, "the long fast highway over the California mountains." "The world above the edge of the foxhole . . . ": refers to Oppen's World War II experience in which a bomb exploded near the foxhole in which he had taken shelter with two other soldiers. The blast killed the other soldiers and wounded GO. The incident is described by David McAleavy in *Ironwood* 26 (309-10).

4. Anniversary Poem

    *Chicago* (Oct., 1973). *Grosseteste Review* 6:1-4 (1973). *Stony Brook* 3-4 (1969). *Jewish-American Literature: An Anthology*. Ed. Abraham Chapman (New York: Mentor/New American Library, 1974). "The Indian girl walking across the desert": a reference to MO. See also "Of This All Things" (NCP, 129).

5. The Translucent Mechanics

    *Grosseteste Review* 6:1-4 (1973). *Iowa Review* 3:1 (Winter 1972). *Ironwood* 1 (Spring 1972). *America a Prophecy: A New Reading of American Poetry from Pre-Columbian Times to the Present*. Eds. Jerome Rothenberg and George Quasha (New York: Random House, 1973). "'and that one's own'": from Charles Tomlinson, "The Picture of J.T. etc." in *A Peopled Landscape* (London: Oxford University Press, 1963), 17.

6. "Silver as / The needle's eye"

*Stony Brook* 3-4 (1969). On image of the needle, see note to poem 1 of this series above. Called "Of the Needle's Eye" in CPF.

7. "O withering seas"

*Iowa Review* 3:1 (Winter 1972). *Ironwood* 1 (Spring 1972). Originally titled "For Jo Miles," after the poet and literary scholar who taught at the University of California, Berkeley (UCSD 16, 23, 17). An earlier draft of the poem reads:

> We arrived in our wet clothes
> And I carried the canoe uphill from the shore
> To a ruined shack in the tall grass
> Where a piano stood, the wood splintered,
> The keyboard gone     Mary swept her hand
> Across the strings as I dropped the canoe
> And the thing rang out
> Over the rocks and the ocean
> Not my poem.     Steinways'
> Poem.     Not mine     A marvelous object is not
>       the marvel
>    of things.     but it rang

8. The Taste

*Sumac* 3:2 (Winter 1971). "In a wind from what were sand dunes": a large portion of San Francisco was built on sand, a fact that contributed to the devastation of the 1906 earthquake, an event alluded to in the previous poem ("In the record of great blows    shocks").

9. The Impossible Poem

*Stony Brook* 3-4 (1969). According to RBDP, the opening lines commemorate a hike that the Oppens took with Charles Amirkhanian and Carol Law, following their marriage in 1969. In a letter to Amirkhanian, Oppen sent an early draft of the poem, calling it "An Abnormal Epithalamium":

> Climbing the peak of Tamalpais one looks to the front
> Not down and sees the loose gravel
>
> And outward streaks of fog in the sky
> And the city shining with the tremendous wrinkles
> In the hills and the winding of the bay
> Behind it, it faces the bent ocean
>
> Niwcomen man     the newcome man . . .
>
>                          (SL, 397-98)

10. But So As by Fire

*Grosseteste Review* 6:1-4 (1973). *Stony Brook* 3-4 (1969). *America a Prophecy: A New Reading of American Poetry from Pre-Columbian Times to the Present.* Eds.

Jerome Rothenberg and George Quasha (New York: Random House, 1973). A version of this poem was published in A. Title derived from 1 Corinthians 3:15, which Oppen quotes in a letter to Diane Meyer:

> 'Mirrors' in that we merely confront now or begin to confront reality
> But in the idea of a mirror is the sense that it gives something back. The
> title comes from Corinthians: 'If any man's work burn, he shall suffer loss;
> yet he himself shall be saved, but so as by fire." (SL, 185)

In the same letter, Oppen included a copy of the poem, with the phrase "Eastern woods" changed to "coastal woods."

EXODUS

In an interview with Kevin Power, Oppen speaks of "Exodus" as follows:

> Yes, it's historical. There's a sort of reference to Adam and Eve, to inno-
> cence. The poem finishes with "Miracle / of." I didn't quite know what
> the miracle would be, but it had to be within the young children.
> (*Montemora* 4 [1978], 203)

# MYTH OF THE BLAZE (1975)

While preparing his *Collected Poems* for publication in 1974, Oppen toyed with the idea of calling the entire volume "Myth of the Blaze." James Laughlin, New Directions's publisher, urged that it be used as a subtitle instead. Oppen agreed in the end but retained the title for the last section of the book. Oppen glosses the title in a letter to Tony Stoneburner:

> of late years, I've become merely dazed, slightly dazed, by coincidence.
> The day before your letter arrived, I'd written down, almost like auto-
> matic writing, the name of the book I've been working on: Myth of
> the Blaze. The Blaze being 'all the Galaxies,' the night-sky, Blake's Tyger.
> (SL, 275)

LATITUDE, LONGITUDE

*Ironwood* 5 (1975). *Poetry Review* 66:1 (1975). *Contemporary American and Australian Poetry*. Ed. Thomas Shapcott (St. Lucia, Queensland, Australia: University of Queensland Press, 1976). Early drafts suggest that this poem was the result of writing a statement (unpublished) on "Open Poetry" (UCSD 16, 24, 1-2). This project, in various drafts (one of which is dated December 27, 1973), contains phrases that appear in numerous poems from *Myth of the Blaze*. The metaphor of the whirlwind from "The Book of Job," the issue of finding speech in "The Speech at Soli," and the definition of poetry in "Latitude, Longitude" can be found here. One draft, crossed out with an 'X' in pen, appears as follows:

> the turn, the cadence, the form, the verse and the
> music, and I want, if I can find it, the essential
> clarity, plain glass
>
> 'far out in the visible, appearance blinks, and is
> behind us. . . . we awake in the same moment to
> ourselves and things'
>
> Strangest of all places, strange as chance, strange as
> luck and its guilt, stranger than that, strange as failure
>
> —the slang word out of the whirl wind, argot out
> of the whirl-winds, I begin to be afraid of the
> clowning hoarded threatening rags of those who
> have refused this heritage
>
> 'The Word comes to existence, and for the last time,
> as language'
>> (UCSD 16, 24, 2)

THE SPEECH AT SOLI
*Grosseteste Review* 10:1-4 (1973). *Ironwood* 5 (1975). *Poetry Review* 66:1 (1975). The poem's title is explained in Oppen's interview with Kevin Power:

> It's a strange poem, a kind of confessional poem. It refers to that back-
> ground of mine, and it's not completely comprehensible. I happened to
> notice that the etymology of the word "solipsism" was the name of a
> place, Soli. The Greeks, apparently, thought that town somewhere in Italy
> to be a very barbarous place. It's a memory of my adolescence. It's a
> memory of those country towns out there and the young girls living
> there. I was thinking of them in the 20's, Fitzgerald's period, and how
> they were caught up in what was then a new freedom. I was thinking of
> the tragedy of all that. (*Montemora* 4 [1978], 200)

"adolescent young girls fall into wells . . . ": variation of lines from RBDP's "Elegies" in *Wells* (New York: Montemora, 1980), n.p. "it will not // cohere . . . ": based on Ezra Pound's Canto CXVI, "Tho' my errors and wrecks lie about me. / And I am not a demigod, / I cannot make it cohere. / If love be not in the house there is nothing." (*The Cantos of Ezra Pound* [New York: New Directions, 1986], 810). When asked by Kevin Power about his allusion to Pound in this poem, Oppen replied: "I was speaking of Pound as against the Populism in my poem, and Pound's words won't cohere, it won't I said, from Pound's damned Bertran de Born." (*Montemora* 4 [1978]: 200). "Friday's footprint": one of numerous references to Defoe's *Robinson Crusoe* throughout GO's work. See also "Of Being Numerous," poems 6, 7, 9.

THE BOOK OF JOB AND A DRAFT OF A POEM TO PRAISE
     THE PATHS OF THE LIVING
*European Judaism* 8:1 (Winter, 1973-74). *Grosseteste Review* 6:1-4 (1973). *Ironwood* 5 (1975). *Poetry Review* 66:1 (1975). *The New Naked Poetry: Recent American Poetry in Open Forms*. Eds. Stephen Berg and Robert Mezey (Indianapolis: Bobbs-Merrill, 1976). A version of section 6 appears as "A Barbarity" in A and CPF. The *Grosseteste Review* version is titled "The Lever The Die The Cam (from the Book of Job)." Portions of this poem appear in a draft titled, "Any Way But Back." See "Selected Unpublished Poems," ( NCP, 342). Dedication: Mickey [Michael] Schwerner, a civil rights activist, cousin of poet Armand Schwerner, who was engaged in voter registration drives in the South. In June 1964 he was beaten and then shot by a white mob in Mississippi, along with his companions, Andrew Goodman and James Chaney. In a letter to Michael Cuddihy, Oppen describes sources quoted in the poem:

> (this the more startling in view of the number of quotes, so many, and none of them from Job      I'd made myself a list of the references, but seem to have lost it—includes "Holderlin, Jabès, Bobrowski, Luther, Montaigne (Florus' trans)
>
>      Luther's is 'seeking a statement' etc. *Middle Kingdom* from Mencius—and others Quotes from memory, which is my disreputable habit— (SL, 264)

"[The] crack trains / of 1918": possibly a reference to the trains that brought Oppen's family to San Francisco from New York that year.

MYTH OF THE BLAZE
*Ironwood* 5 (1975). *Poetry Review* 66:1 (1975). *Contemporary American and Australian Poetry*. Ed. Thomas Shapcott (St. Lucia, Queensland, Australia: University of Queensland Press, 1976). "Wyatt's / lyric and Rezi's . . . ": a reference to Sir Thomas Wyatt's lyric, "They Flee from Me That Sometime Did Me Seek," and to poems of Charles Reznikoff. In a letter to Reznikoff's editor, Milton Hindus, Oppen remembers the final days of World War II:

> . . . found myself trapped in a fox-hole, slightly injured, and with no

apparent means of escape, certainly no possibility until night-fall. I waited, I think, some ten hours, and during those hours Wyatt's little poem—'they flee from me . . . .' and poem after poem of Rezi's ran thru my mind over and over, these poems seemed to fill all the space around me and I wept and wept. (SL, 338)

"[Eyes] / of the Tyger": a reference to William Blake's "Tyger," from *Songs of Experience*. See note to book's title above.

INLET

*Prospice* 1 (Nov. 1973). *Sumac* 3:2 (Winter 1971). Written while the Oppens were spending the summer in Maine. "*Shepherds are good people let them sing.*" From George Herbert, "Jordan" I, line 11. GO changes Herbert from "honest people" to "good people":

> Shepherds are honest people; let them sing:
> Riddle who list, for me, and pull for Prime:
> I envie no mans nightingale or spring;
> Nor let them punish me with losse of rime,
>     Who plainly say, *My God, My King.*

> *The Works of George Herbert.* Ed. F. E. Hutchinson
> (Oxford: Clarendon Press, 1964), 57.

SEMITE

*American Poetry Review* 3:5 (Sept.-Oct. 1974). Originally titled "Reznikoff's Reading: The Quiet Earth Rises" (UCSD 6, 24, 14). "[G]uilts // of the foxhole": a reference to Oppen's World War II experiences. See note to "Myth of the Blaze" and David McAleavy's "Remarks Towards Autobiography: An Interview with David McAleavy" (*Ironwood* 26 [Fall 1985]: 309). See also ML, 178. On Oppen's response to his Jewishness, see SL, pp. 270-72. "[a] planet the size // of a table top": John Taggart suggests that this is a reference to Wallace Stevens's poem, "The Planet on the Table" (Wallace Stevens, *Collected Poems*. [New York: Knopf, 1968], 532). John Taggart, "Walk-Out: Rereading George Oppen," *Chicago Review* 44:2 (1998): 47. "my distances neither Roman // nor barbarian." Variations on these lines appear in drafts to numerous poems of this period. See also "The Lighthouses" (NCP, 256) where "distances" becomes "heritage."

THE LITTLE PIN: FRAGMENT

*American Poetry Review* 4:2 (Mar.-Apr. 1975). "small pin of the wind and the rayne": presumably refers to the 15th-century "Western Wind," a favorite lyric of

Oppen's quoted in "O Western Wind" (NCP, 74).

> O Western wind, when will thou blow
> The small rain down can rain.
> Christ! if my love were in my arms
> And I in my bed again
>
> (SL, 147)

"small pin of the wind and the rayne": seems to be a conflation of lines in several Shakespeare plays. Given Oppen's reference to "High seas of history . . . Stagecraft / Statecraft . . . " the "small pin" could come from Richard II's speech in Richard II, III.ii:

> For God's sake let us sit upon the ground
> And tell sad stories of the death of kings!
> How some have been deposed, some slain in war,
> Some haunted by the ghosts they have deposed,
> Some poisoned by their wives, some sleeping killed—
> All murdered; for within the hollow crown
> That rounds the mortal temples of a king
> Keeps Death his court; and there the antic sits,
> Scoffing his state and grinning at his pomp;
> Allowing him a breath, a little scene,
> To monarchize, be feared, and kill with looks;
> Infusing him with self and vain conceit,
> As if this flesh which walls about our life
> Were brass impregnable; and humored thus,
> Comes at the last, and with a little pin
> Bores through his castle wall, and farewell king!
>
> (155–70)

The "wind and the rayne" refers to the Clown's speech in the epilogue to *Twelfth Night*:

> When that I was a little tiny boy,
>     With hey ho, the wind and the rain,
> A foolish thing was but a toy,
>     For the rain it raineth every day.
>
> (378–11)

A version of the song is also performed by the Fool in *King Lear* III.ii (74–77).

THE LIGHTHOUSES

A variant version, "Gift: the Gifted," appeared in *Ironwood* 5 (1975). Dedication: to Louis Zukofsky, Oppen's friend and Objectivist colleague. The two had been close during their early days but became estranged in later life. The opening lines are derived from Zukofsky's interview with L.S. Dembo, who asks the poet "[what] do you mean, you got rid of epistemology in Bottom? The work seems to me to be all epistemology," to which Zukofsky replies: "'The questions are their own answers.' You want to say 'yes,' say 'yes'; you want to say 'no,' say 'no.' It's a useless argument" (CL, 215). In her interview with Dennis Young, MO identifies "all my fathers" as referring to Oppen's poetic mentors and teachers, "Pound, Zukofsky, Blake." (*Iowa Review* [Fall 1988]: 30). "the breaking of nations": may refer to the Middle East strife between Israel and the Palestinians in the early 1970s.

WHO SHALL DOUBT

In a letter to John Taggart of 1974, Oppen quotes the opening lines of the poem, adding "This is indeed the law and the prophets. It can happen in the poem. Perhaps this should have been the meaning of 'objectivism'" (SL, 290).

TO THE POETS: TO MAKE MUCH OF LIFE

Most of this poem reappears in P, "To Make Much" (NCP, 271).

TWO ROMANCE POEMS

*Transatlantic Review* 52 (Autumn 1975). "bright light of shipwreck": quoted from "Of Being Numerous," poem 9 (NCP, 167). "Res Publica:" Latin: the public thing or way.

# PRIMITIVE (1978)

*Primitive*, Oppen's last book, was published in 1978 by Black Sparrow Press in a small, letter-press edition. Several of the poems were reprinted as a series under the title, "*If It All Went Up in Smoke*," in *Voices Within the Ark: The Modern Jewish Poets*. Eds. Howard Schwartz and Anthony Rudolf (New York: Avon, 1980). Although Oppen was becoming widely known, the question of fame recurs several times in the book. Sherwood Anderson's "*we wanted to know // if we were any good // out there*" is a leitmotif as GO contemplates the resilience of poetry in a lifetime of social engagement.

At the time of *Primitive*'s publication, GO was seventy years old and was beginning to show signs of the Alzheimer's disease that ultimately claimed his life

in 1984. Although the disease was not diagnosed until 1982, there is evidence that
he was becoming increasingly disoriented and forgetful. Writing to JOD, GO says,
"On a little path fifty yards long from here to the road (and which I've been over
a hundred times) I somehow got lost!" (SL, 339). At least one poem in the book,
"Disasters," indirectly alludes to his disorientation (in its early manuscript version,
the poem is titled "Senility"). Due to these symptoms, MO became more active-
ly involved in the preparation and typing of the manuscript. Her handwriting
appears on numerous manuscript drafts and lists of poems to be included. The
book's last poem acknowledges her sustaining presence—and that of others—by
inverting T. S. Eliot's final lines of "The Love Song of J. Alfred Prufrock" to read

> lights have entered
> us it is a music more powerful
>
> than music
>
> till other voices wake
> us or we drown

A POLITICAL POEM
*Ironwood* 12 (Fall 1978).

DISASTERS
*American Poetry Review* 5:5 (Sept.-Oct. 1976). *Grosseteste Review* 10: 1-4
(Summer 1977). *Ironwood* 9 (1977). *New Wilderness Letter (Poetry Supplement)*
1:3-4 (Dec. 1977-Jan. 1978). *Voices Within the Ark* (cf. headnote). At one point, GO
titled the poem "Senility: A Poem of Politics" (UCSD 16, 26, 5). "[Legislators] // of
the unacknowledged // world": a variation on Shelley's phrase, "poets are the unac-
knowledged legislators of the world" from his "Defense of Poetry" (1821). "*it is
dreary / to descend // and be a stranger*": according to John Taggart ("Walk-Out:
Rereading George Oppen," *Chicago Review* 44:2 [1998]: 59), this line is from
Nathaniel Hawthorne's *House of the Seven Gables*:

> Why are poets apt to choose their mates, not for any similarity of poet-
> ic endowment, but for qualities which might make the happiness of the
> rudest handicraftsman, as well as that of the ideal craftsman of the spir-
> it? Because, probably, at his highest elevation, the poet needs no human
> intercourse, but he finds it dreary to descend, and be a stranger.
> (Nathaniel Hawthorne, *The House of the Seven Gables* [New York:
> Penguin, 1984], 141.)

"*we wanted to know // if we were any good*": from Sherwood Anderson, "Song of
the Soul of Chicago" (*Mid-American Chants* [New York: John Lane, 1918], 62-

63): "We want to see if we are any good out here, we Americans from all over hell." See also 1973 letter to Dan Gerber (SL, 260-61). Sarah: in Genesis, the wife of Abraham and mother of Isaac. "my lost / sister": a reference to Oppen's sister, Libby, who died in 1960.

THE POEM
Ironwood 9 (1977). Voices Within the Ark (cf. headnote). "Tyger": one of several references to Blake's "Tyger" from Songs of Experience that occur in GO's late poems.

TO MAKE MUCH
Ironwood 9 (1977). Voices Within the Ark (cf. headnote). This poem includes most of "To the Poets: To Make Much of Life," from Myth of the Blaze (NCP, 260). "it was no dream all's wild / out there": from Sir Thomas Wyatt's 16th-century lyric, "They Flee From Me That Sometime Did Me Seek."

WAKING WHO KNOWS
Ironwood 9 (1977). Voices Within the Ark (cf. headnote).

IF IT ALL WENT UP IN SMOKE
Ironwood 9 (1977). Voices Within the Ark (cf. headnote). "that smoke / would remain": Oppen's adaptation of Heraclitus's Fragment #7, translated by G.S. Kirk: "If all existing things were to become smoke the nostrils would distinguish them." (G.S. Kirk, Heraclitus: The Cosmic Fragments. New York: Cambridge University Press, 1959. p. 232.) Oppen quotes the fragment in his essay "The Mind's Own Place": "'If it all went up in smoke' that smoke would remain."

THE TONGUES
Ironwood 9 (1977). Voices Within the Ark (cf. headnote).

GOLD ON OAK LEAVES
American Poetry Review 7:3 (May-June 1978). Montemora 4 (1978). The opening lines, "gold said her golden // young poem . . . " refer to an early poem by MO, written when she and GO started hitchhiking across the United States. In the version of the poem published in American Poetry Review (titled "Gold on Oak Leaves Said Young") the opening lines read as follows:

> Mary's poem    vision
> image the pure body
>
> of idea rang in the young

voice but for the gold
light I would drown

(in the gold
light) as many dreams

as dreamers on this salt and sleepless

sea guilts . . .

THE NATURAL
*Ironwood* 9 (1977). *Montemora* 4 (1978). The opening lines referring to "*the fog /
coming up in the fields*" are variations on "The Forms of Love" (NCP, 106).

STRANGE ARE THE PRODUCTS
*Montemora* 3 (1977).

NEIGHBORS
*Montemora* 4 (1978).

TILL OTHER VOICES WAKE US
The title and final lines invoke T. S. Eliot's "The Love Song of J. Alfred Prufrock,"
which concludes as follows:

> We have lingered in the chambers of the sea
> By sea-girls wreathed with seaweed red and brown
> Till human voices wake us, and we drown.
>
> T. S. Eliot. *The Complete Poems and Plays, 1909–1950* (New York:
> Harcourt, Brace & World, 1962), 7.

"adolescence with my father / in France": refers to the European trip that Oppen
took with his parents prior to entering college. "Brooklyn, 1929": refers to the
period in which he composed the first poems of the book that was to become DS.

# UNCOLLECTED PUBLISHED POEMS

Included in this section are all the poems published by George Oppen that do not appear in CP or P. Because GO often used lines or stanzas in several poems or else published poems with variant titles, it is sometimes difficult to distinguish between collected and uncollected poems. Lines from "A Barbarity," for example, appear in "The Book of Job," yet by printing it separately in A, GO appears to have thought of it as a discrete poem. "Monument" is the title of a poem that also appeared in CP but, with the exception of a few words, it differs entirely from that printed in this section. In such cases, I have attempted to note where other variant versions appear, referring where possible to drafts located in the UCSD GO collection. For a full account of GO's publishing history, see David McAleavy, "A Bibliography of the Works of George Oppen," *Paideuma* 10.1 (Spring 1981): 155-69.

## POEMS 1932–1933

DISCRETE SERIES I-III
*Poetry* 39. 4 (Jan. 1932): 198-99. A fourth poem, "Cat Boat," a variant of "The mast . . ." in DS, was also included in this group of poems. Also published in *Ironwood* 13:2 (Fall 1985): 69-71. Other poems omitted from DS can be found among the "Selected Unpublished Poems": "The pigeons fly . . . "; "Preceded by mounted police . . . "; "Steamer at the pier"; "A laced gaiter . . . ".

[BRAIN]
*Active Anthology*, ed. Ezra Pound (London: Faber and Faber, 1933), 217. Also included in a privately printed version of DS sent to Charles Reznikoff (UCSD 16, 20, 1), as well as in *Ironwood* 13:2 (Fall 1985): 72.

## POEMS 1960–1981

THE BIBLICAL TREE
*Poetry* 95.4 (Jan. 1960): 239 (UCSD 16, 26, 22).

MONUMENT
*San Francisco Review* 7 (Dec. 1960): 72 (UCSD 16, 26, 23). Differs substantially from "Monument" in TW, (NCP, 145).

MEMORY AT 'THE MODERN'
*Elizabeth* VI (Oct. 1963), 1 (UCSD 16, 26, 25). "'No other taste shall change this'": refers to Ezra Pound's Canto IV:

> "It is Cabestan's heart in the dish"
> "It is Cabestan's heart in the dish?
> "No other taste shall change this."

> *The Cantos of Ezra Pound* (New York: New Directions, 1986), 13.

A PREFACE
*Poetry* 111.3 (Dec. 1967): 173.

VOYAGE
*Friendly Local Press* 1.5 (1968): 31.

FROM THE FRIENDLY LOCAL PRESS
*Friendly Local Press* 1.5 (1968): 31.

THE STUDENTS GATHER
*Promethean* 16.1 (1968-69): 7.

EPIGRAM
*Bricoleur* (Sept. 1969), n.p. *Stony Brook* 3-4 (1969): 22.

A MODERN INCIDENT
*Stony Brook* 3-4 (1969): 24.

THE THEOLOGICAL QUESTION
*Stony Brook* 3-4 (1969): 24.

[ASTRAY OVER EARTH . . . ]
Translation of Parmenides' "Moon fragment," in Alexander P. D. Mourelatos, *The Route of Parmenides: A Study of Word, Image, and Argument in the Fragments* (New Haven: Yale University Press, 1970), 225.

THE SONG
*Elizabeth* XV (May 1970): 46. James L. Weil, *My Music Bent* (New Rochelle, NY:

Elizabeth Press, 1978), 53. *Chicago* (Oct. 1973), n.p. A (n.p.). Included in "Song, the Winds of Downhill," (NCP, 220).

A POEM ABOUT THE GARDEN
*Ironwood* 1 (March 1972): 14. On a photocopy of the published poem, GO corrected the last line ("a flower, and been a stranger") to read "a flower, and become a stranger" (UCSD 16, 24, 34).

A BARBARITY
A (n.p.). Included in "The Book of Job . . . " part 6 (NCP, 240). In A, "weird" spelled "wierd."

ARTIST
*Iowa Review* 6.3-4 (Summer-Fall 1975): 45-46.

THE LAW OF POETRY
*Iowa Review* 6.3-4 (Summer-Fall 1975): 46.

[BEAUTIFUL AS THE SEA]
Published as a broadside in the "Poetry in Public Places" project, sponsored by the American International Sculptor's Symposiums, Inc., 1976. Parts of the poem appear in "Two Romance Poems" (NCP, 261).

[SYMPATHY . . . ]
*Tractor* 6 (1975): 64.

TO FIND A WAY
*Ironwood* 5 (1975): 28. *Poetry Review* (London) 66.1 (1975): 6. Several lines appear in "Semite" (NCP, 251).

GIFT: THE GIFTED
*Ironwood* 5 (1975): 38-39. *Poetry Review* (London), 66:1 (1975). Several lines appear in "The Lighthouses" (NCP, 256).

EAGLES AND ALONE
*Grosseteste Review* 10. 1-4 (Summer 1977): 203-4. A variant, "Fear," appears in *American Poetry Review* 5.5 (Sept.-Oct. 1976): 14.

IMAGE
*Montemora* 3 (1977): 6-7. *Grosseteste Review* 10.1-4 (Summer 1977): 198-99. Several lines appear in "Populist" (NCP, 276).

In Memoriam Charles Reznikoff

Printed on the back cover of Charles Reznikoff, *Poems 1937–1975: Volume II of the Complete Poems*. Ed. Seamus Cooney (Santa Barbara: Black Sparrow Press, 1977). Added to MS draft: "unsigned: as tho it came from—everyone. As it should. And maybe will. When they wake."

[he de dark]

Valentine included in Mary Oppen, ML, 119.

Probity

*Montemora* 4 (1978): 240.

The Whirl Wind Must

*American Poetry Review* 7.3 (May-June 1978): 19.

The Poem

*Paideuma* 10.1 (Spring 1981). In this special issue devoted to GO, "The Poem" appears on the title page, followed by "George Oppen, 1980." *Orange Export Lts. 1969–1986*. Ed. Emmanuel Hocquard and Raquel (Paris: Flammarion, 1986): 251. Included in a letter to Claude Royet-Journoud, Sept. 26, 1981, thought by RBDP to be GO's last piece of correspondence (SL, 424–25, n. 21.)

# SELECTED UNPUBLISHED POEMS

Poems in this section have been selected from GO's manuscripts and correspondence located at the University of California, San Diego. Although I am using the term "unpublished" here, several of them have seen print in one form or another. Prior to publishing *Discrete Series*, GO sent a typed manuscript of the proposed volume to Charles Reznikoff that appears among that poet's papers at UCSD. This is the only known example of a manuscript from GO's earlier life, the rest of his papers having been destroyed or lost at some point during the 1950s. When GO edited DS for publication by The Objectivist Press, several of these poems were omitted and appear here. In 1989, RBDP edited a selection of previously unpublished poems for *Sulfur* magazine. Most of these are reprinted here, rather than in the uncollected published section, since their editing was not done by Oppen directly. In some cases, these versions differ from those in *Sulfur*.

GO rarely dated his poems, and establishing even the most general period of composition is sometimes difficult. In some cases, reference to a current event will provide a date. The poem "Bill before his death" had to have been published at least *after* William Carlos Williams's death in 1963. "Wheelers and Dealers" was included in a letter to JOD from the early 1960s. "The Poem" was typed on a sheet of paper containing a preliminary list of poems for "Myth of the Blaze," which concluded the 1975 CP. Wherever possible, I have indicated the general period in which a poem was composed, often on the basis of a hunch relating to data on the accompanying page. But since GO often added material to pages previously typed or written upon—sometimes years later—it is not always clear that a given piece of contextual information applies to an entire page. Poems typed upon paper with a Brooklyn letterhead might suggest composition prior to 1966 when the Oppens left for California, yet GO brought reams of this letterhead paper with him that he continued to use in the West.

Since these poems have been selected from manuscripts that are often extensively corrected and emended, I have had to make some difficult choices with regard to words and spacing. It is rare to find an Oppen poem in draft form that does not have some marginal corrections or crossings-out. GO also wrote in an almost unintelligible hand, which has made deciphering certain corrections difficult. Given these limitations, I have tried to ascertain the last version upon which GO worked, often by looking through a dozen or more separate drafts. Since GO, often as not, condensed or shortened the poem, it was not always easy to assume that the fullest or longest version was the definitive one. In some cases, a poem was sent to a correspondent in fair copy, and assuming that this represents a kind of "publication," I have tended to favor these "correspondent" versions. At the same time, it was not uncommon for GO to return to poems long after composition and continue fiddling with them. Thus this section should be regarded not only as a "selected" unpublished poems but a "provisional selection" as well.

# POEMS FROM THE 1930s

[THE PIGEONS FLY . . . ]
Ca. late 1930s. S, 23 (UCSD 16, 20, 1). Included in a typescript of DS sent to Charles Reznikoff (hereafter called "Reznikoff typescript").

[PRECEDED BY MOUNTED POLICE]
Included in a letter to Ezra Pound, March 10, 1934, with the comment "Poem with this—sorry I didn't get it in to replace Civil war photo," the latter a reference to a poem in DS (NCP, 21). See letter to Pound in SL, 5.

[STEAMER AT THE PIER]
Reznikoff typescript (UCSD 16, 20, 1).

# POEMS FROM THE 1950S TO THE 1970S

FROM UP-STATE
Ca. 1960. Included in a typescript of "Another Language of New York," an earlier version of "A Language of New York" in TW.

MEMORY OF OARS
Ca. late 1950s (UCSD 16, 20, 46; 16, 27, 72). Located in a folder labeled "Some San Francisco Poems," typed in Acapulco, Mexico, and dated Jan. 1960. "A rocket into space" that displaces "home" could refer to the Russian Sputnik satellite that was launched in October 1957.

THE AMALGAMATED
Ca. 1963. S, 28 (UCSD 16, 27, 11).

GENERATION OF DRIVERS
Sent to *San Francisco Review*, Jan. 1959. S, 25 (UCSD 16, 1, 1).

THE NEW PEOPLE
Ca. late 1950s. Excluded from TW (UCSD 16, 21, 42).

ACAPULCO.
Ca. late 1950s (UCSD 16, 20, 46). Included in MS sent to *Poetry* 1960. Later included in "Return" (NCP, 47).

NEAR THE BEGINNING
Late 1950s. Typed on same page as "Acapulco" (UCSD 16, 20, 46).

BELVEDERE
Late 1950s, omitted from TW. "Belvedere": small, upscale town north of San Francisco, located on Richardson Bay, where members of the Oppen family lived at various times.

BRONX ZOO
Ca. early 1960s. S, 32 (UCSD 17, 4, 17). In a letter to JOD Oppen asks to exclude from TW.

[BILL BEFORE HIS DEATH]
Ca. 1963. S, 34 (UCSD 16, 27, 22). William Carlos Williams died on March 4, 1963, after a series of strokes that impeded his speech and movements.

11/22/63
Written on the day that John F. Kennedy was assassinated (UCSD 16, 1, 4).

A CULTURAL TRIUMPH
n.d. S, 31 (UCSD 16, 27, 39). Excluded from TW. Holograph note at bottom of MS: "Quote from Hugh Kenner in 'Poetry.'"

VISIT (1)
Ca. early 1960s (UCSD 16, 21, 42). Excluded from TW. GO and MO first visited France in 1929. In one draft, the last six lines appear as an independent poem, "Self-Awareness at a Dinner":

> It is true, as someone
> Said, I think I am
> Adam. I do not want to know
> Where the animals
> Have already been named
> I want only
> To go home.

FLIGHT 162
Ca. early 1960s. S, 32 (UCSD 16, 27, 66).

CHURCH INTERIOR
Ca. early 1960s (UCSD 16, 27, 36).

MAUDIT
Ca. early 1960s.

MOUNT DESERT ISLAND
Included in letter to JOD, July 1964 (UCSD 16, 1, 7). Mount Desert Island is located in Penobscot Bay off the coast of Maine and was a favorite summer destination for the Oppens.

MOTHER AND CHILD
Ca. 1962-65 (UCSD 16, 21, 42). Excluded from TW. A variant called "Young Mother" suggests that this poem is based on a painting by Goya. The second stanza of "Young Mother" reads as follows:

Outward from forgotten roots,
Best forgotten, growing
Like the black branch in Goya's print
Out into space, the most living
Green tip fed by a sap
The great black mass brings it, leafing
From the thin twig in new space.

WHEELERS AND DEALERS: THE THEORY OF GAMES
Ca. 1963. S, 34. In a letter to JOD, GO says, "'Wheelers and Dealers' is not an
attack on you, tho I heard the phrase from you. The poem means to acknowledge
this abstract way of thought as perfectly contemporary, perhaps the only way for
a clear intelligence to go, barring a fanatic stand" (UCSD 16, 1, 4). The variant
published in *Sulfur* 25 includes an epigraph by Rilke, "The world is becoming
invisible," crossed out in this version.

THE PHONEMES
Ca. early 1960s. S, 35 (UCSD 16, 28, 77).

LIGHT OF DAY
Holograph on typescript indicates that the phrase, "'Lovely enchanting language,
sugar-cane,/ Hony of roses——'" is from George Herbert, "The Forerunners." The
passage "'The stubborn rhetorical/passion'" is ascribed to Erich Auerbach. A vari-
ant, "To the Dancer," reads as follows:

The sun moving down toward evening
Lit half of the table top
And two chairs

In the cafe, making all of us
Happy that the event
Was so large which had caused this

Among the chairs, the diminished point
On the stage.

NATION
Written in Acapulco and sent to *Poetry*, 1960. S, 29 (UCSD 16, 20, 46). Some lines
included in "Philai Te Kou Philai," in TW (NCP, 97).

VISIT (2)
Ca. 1960 (UCSD 16, 21, 42). In a MS of TW, a poem appears, "Wedding," which

begins "We talked, the two fathers ..." Lewis could be Louis Zukofsky, who lived in Brooklyn Heights and was visited by GO during the 1960s.

## THE EXTREME
Ca. late 1960s. I, 26. (UCSD 16, 23, 15) Found in a folder containing poems published in SNE.

## [PRESSES WERE BUSY ENOUGH]
Ca. late 1960s. I, 26. Found in folder containing poems published in SNE. Quite possibly this is the conclusion to "The Extreme," based on typeface and proximity in the folder.

## VOLKSWAGEN
Ca. late 1960s. I, 26 (UCSD 16, 20, 47). Oppen is referring to the complicity between the Volkswagen automobile factory and the Nazi regime during World War II.

## THE DOG
Ca. early 1960s. This is the second of several versions of poems by the Bengali poet Buddhadeva Bose, who was a friend of the Oppens during their time in Brooklyn, 1960-66. See also "To Memory" (NCP, 86). In a letter to JOD, GO speaks of seeing Bose's self-translated poems in the journal *Kavita*: "I was immensely moved by them and set myself to put them into more idiomatic English." (UCSD 16, 1, 3). According to another letter to JOD, Oppen felt that, although Bose agreed to the revision, he (Bose) was "surely not happy with it" (SL, 378, n. 6).

## ORPHEUS
(UCSD 16, 1, 4). Initially titled "The Albano," named after a ship.

## VALENTINE
Late 1960s. This poem is outlined in pencil in the shape of a heart. Dating for this and the following three poems is based on shared emphasis on the pronoun and by the San Francisco Polk Street letterhead that occurs on the last of the poems, "Say."

## US
Late 1960s.

## SEMANTIC
Late 1960s.

SAY

Late 1960s. Below the poem, a handwritten copyright mark, followed by the poet's name, typed. A note, typed, in brackets follows: "[note to the organizers of this project: the copyright notice must be included because this poem is unprinted, and because the notice is appropriate to the spirit of this poem]." It is unknown to what "project" this refers.

A WIND MAKES UP

Alternate title crossed out: "The Town and Down."

WHAT WILL HAPPEN

Alternate title crossed out in MS, "Antinomian."

THE RESOLVE

Alternate title, crossed out in draft, "The Mobilization."

THE SPACE

Typed at the bottom of the MS: "Blake could make an epic of 'Mental fight' because he held that the vegetative world, the world of experience was created by man's imagination—a fight, therefore, not less important than the battle of the angels—"

ANY WAY BUT BACK

Ca. 1972–75. S, 35–36. A shorter version, included in a letter to an unknown recipient, includes the comment: "I wrote this poem (tentatively) as poem to close the new book—the title from the story I quoted to you—"The "new book" was apparently, "Myth of the Blaze." Several lines suggest those in "The Book of Job . . ." (NCP, 240). "[trains] of 1918": refers to the Oppen family's migration to San Francisco from New York in that year.

THE POWERS

Ca. 1972–75. S, 37–38.(UCSD 16, 24, 2). Portions of this poem appear in "Semite" (NCP, 251), "The Lighthouses" (NCP, 256), and "To Find a Way" (NCP, 302)

ALL THIS STRANGENESS

Ca. 1972–75. S, 38–40. (UCSD 16, 24, 2). Autograph note on manuscript by Oppen says "Not in Collected."

A DREAM OF POLITICS

Ca. 1972–75. S, 40-41. (UCSD 16, 24, 16, Version "C"). GO note on the manuscript page: "Write [Peter] Glassgold to omit this." Another note reads "(perhaps isn't in ND ms)." Peter Glassgold is the editor at New Directions who worked with GO on the

1975 CP.

THE RESISTANCE
Several drafts for this poem exist, one of which is titled "The Rebellious One"
and is dedicated to "Diane." It opens as follows:

> In effect she has written a body of poetry. Partisan
> She condemns
> Only the victorious and gives herself
> To the defeated and wanders in the fields
> Of faith.

[A WOMAN, SAID DIANE . . . ]
Ca. 1969. "Diane" is Diane (Andy) Meyer, the poet's niece. The poem responds to
a 1969 letter from Meyer that includes the remark, "A man sees the ocean takes
a boat, an oar or a sail and grapples with it. I have spent my life hanging over the
edge not wanting to use the tools" (SL, 398-99). In a letter to Meyer, GO says:

> It is true a man will grab an oar. Any stick to beat a father with. What
> is the feminine. The love of standing still, of hugging to oneself. Of con-
> taining? It is not a feminine culture, it is very hard for women. Terribly,
> terribly hard. (SL, 185)

THE POEM
Ca. 1972-75. The typescript includes a handwritten list of poems, one of which
is "Who Shall Doubt" from *Myth of the Blaze* (1972-75).

THE DREAM
S, 41 (UCSD 26, 27, 55). RBDP, in an editorial note to the *Sulfur* 25 publication,
states that this poem was "explicitly excluded from *Primitive.*"

MARY
Ca. 1972-75. Lines suggest the last poem in P (see NCP, 286):

> lights have entered
> us it is a music more powerful
>
> than music
>
> till other voices wake
> us or we drown

# INDEX OF TITLES AND FIRST LINES

# CD INDEX

from *Myth of the Blaze* (1972-1975)

from *Primitive* (1978)

Total time: 64 minutes and 40 seconds

All audio tracks copyright © 2008 Linda Oppen. Tracks 1-9, 16-23 were recorded by the Academy of American Poets at the Guggenheim Museum, New York, April 9, 1964. Tracks 10-15 were recorded at San Francisco State University, February 19, 1963. Tracks 18 and 34 were recorded at Shippensburg University, September 17, 1974. Track 24 was recorded at the Polytechnic of Central London, May 25-27, 1973. Tracks 25, 29-30, 32, and 37-40 were recorded by Verna Gillis (with Alan Austin and Anne Becker of Watershed Tapes) in Brooklyn, New York, April 28-29, 1979. Tracks 26-28, 31, 33, and 35-36 were recorded at San Francisco State University, May 3, 1972.

The publisher would like to thank Richard Swigg for his monumental efforts in compiling this recording. Thanks also to John Taggart for providing the Shippensburg reading, and to Steve Dickison at the San Francisco Poetry Center for providing the SFSU readings.